WHY STUDY THE PAST

WHY STUDY THE PAST?

The Quest for the Historical Church

Rowan Williams

WILLIAM B. EERDMANS PUBLISHING COMPANY
GRAND RAPIDS, MICHIGAN

© 2005 Rowan Williams

First published 2005 in the United Kingdom by
Darton, Longman and Todd Ltd, London

This edition published 2005 in the United States of America by
Wm. B. Eerdmans Publishing Company
255 Jefferson Ave. S.E., Grand Rapids, Michigan 49503
www.eerdmans.com

Printed and bound in Great Britain

10 09 08 07 06 05   5 4 3 2 1

ISBN 0-8028-2990-2

The contents of this book were originally presented in May 2003
as part of the Sarum Theological Lectures series.

CONTENTS

Introduction   I

1 MAKING HISTORY: What Do We Expect from the
  Past?   4

2 RESIDENT ALIENS: The Identity of the Early
  Church   32

3 GRACE ALONE: Continuity and Novelty in the
  Reformation Era   60

4 HISTORY AND RENEWAL: The Records of the
  Body of Christ   88

Notes   115

Index   126

INTRODUCTION

This book started life as a series of lectures given in May 2003 in Salisbury Cathedral, under the auspices of Sarum College; I am very grateful to the College for this opportunity, and to all who attended (braving a variety of temperatures and acoustical challenges), those who pursued questions and discussion, and all at the Cathedral who so generously assisted in mounting the events (and dealing with temperatures and acoustical challenges). The present text is a good deal longer than the original lectures, and this has given me the chance to clarify various ideas and to respond indirectly to some points raised in discussion.

Essentially, I am trying to make three points. First, history is a set of stories we tell in order to understand better who we are and the world we're now in; as a written affair, it is never just a catalogue of things that happen to have happened. It is bound to be making judgements about the importance of what it deals with, and often – always? – has some element of moral judgement not far below the surface. We start telling the story to get a better definition of who we are or of what the subject is that we're describing: history helps us define things. Good history makes us think again about the definition of things we thought we understood pretty well, because it engages not just with what is familiar but with what is strange. It recognises that 'the past is a foreign country' as well as being *our* past.

All this applies to the history of the Church as it does to other institutions. Church history becomes popular as an exercise when the definition of the Church seems less clear than it had been or needs defending against what are thought to be mistaken definitions. So when we look at how Church history has been written, we shall see people trying to establish more plainly what sort of thing the Church is. Sometimes they think they can do this only by resorting to a sort of conspiracy theory: once it was All Right, then it was taken over by Greek philosophy, Latin legalism, the Pope, patriarchy, monarchism or whatever. But the challenge is still to come up with one story that has some continuity. The book begins, then, with a look at some examples of all this, from different periods.

But this opens up a second, deeper question. The Church claims to be the most comprehensive human society there is – the new human race in embryo. And it claims this because of its belief that it is established not by any human process grounded in and limited by events, cultures and so on, but by God's activity. For someone trying to write the history of the Church as a Christian believer, the challenge is to trace the ways in which the Church has demonstrated its divine origin – or at least has tried to avoid formulae and practices that obscure the claim to divine origin. The two middle chapters of the book examine some of the ways in which, in the earliest centuries of the Church and in the tormented debates of the Reformation era, people's understanding of the Church was shaped by these concerns, in their attitude to past and present. I have tried to show how, as we look at these periods, we can see coming into light some of the main points that have to be thought about in any theory of what the Church is that grows from the belief that it derives from God.

So I am looking for a way of reading Church history that is theologically sensitive. This does not mean allowing theological interests to settle historical questions or pretending that you should not pay attention to human motives and social or political conditioning when you look at the Christian past: good theology does not come from bad history. We have to admit that some of the Church histories of the past are indeed bad history because they move too quickly from theology and spirituality to the shape of past events. But – and here is the third point – the Christian believes that Christians past and present (and future for that matter) are all bound up together in the Body of Christ, the community in which each contributes something unique to the life of all. And this means that the Christian will be looking and listening in his or her study of Christian history for what feeds and nourishes belief now; they will not simply write off the past as a record of sad or cruel or stupid error (however much there may be of all those). There will be an element of expectation: we shall emerge from the study of the past with some greater fullness of Christian maturity.

This last goes against the grain of a lot of our current practice, whether we call ourselves traditionalist or progressive. As I shall be saying more than once, traditionalists sometimes miss the point because they don't expect to be surprised by the past; progressives miss the point because they don't expect to be interested or questioned by it. And in a cultural setting where a sensible understanding of history is not much encouraged, it isn't surprising if religious people can be as much at sea as anyone else in coming to terms with the past.

This book has been written in the hope of encouraging people to look at Christian history expecting to be surprised and questioned. It tries to cover a lot of ground and I apologise for the times when I have taken something for granted that is not going to be familiar or have given a misleadingly simplified account of hugely complicated processes. On every page I am indebted to those who do serious history and do it in such a way as to surprise and challenge. The discussions that follow would have been very different without the example, friendship and help of people like Lewis Ayres, Tim Barnes, Kate Cooper, Brian Golding, Judith Herrin, Sean Hughes, Elizabeth Macfarlane, Judith Maltby, Diarmaid MacCulloch and Karen Torjesen. Thanks to them all and to many other colleagues and companions; and, as always, to Jane.

ROWAN WILLIAMS
Lambeth, Advent 2004

MAKING HISTORY:
WHAT DO WE EXPECT
FROM THE PAST?

I

When people set out to prove that nothing has changed, you can normally be sure that something quite serious *has*. The very fact of feeling you need to show that things are the same implies that there has been an unsettlement of what was once taken for granted. When there is no awareness of things changing, certain questions are not asked; what exists seems obvious, natural. If you have to *prove* that it's natural, you may succeed or you may not, but there has been a sort of loss of innocence. It has become plain that you can no longer take for granted that everyone really knows what is obvious or natural.

Children don't on the whole write autobiographies. It is said that when the Catholic biblical scholar Ronald Knox was a boy of four and was asked what he did if he couldn't sleep, he said, 'I lie awake and think about the past'; but it is safe to assume that he is a bit unusual. We start reflecting on how to tell the story of our lives when we've become a little more aware of how different we've become from what we remember. The same sure-ly applies to the stories we tell of our common past: to history. So far from history being an innocent attempt to list events in a sort of neutral space, history tries to identify more clearly what its own subject is. In that sense, there is no universal history. 'What happened in 1066?' looks like a simple question with a simple correct answer – the Battle of Hastings. But that takes for granted that we all know what story we are telling: the story of who governed the loose coalition of local principalities that came to be called England. All sorts of other things happened in 1066; and for chroniclers in – say – medieval Indonesia, it may well be that 1066 (or rather the equivalent in local numeration) was a particularly uneventful year. Even '1066' as a date tells us that this is a story set in the Christian world, a story whose shape is in some way moulded by events that happened in Palestine just over 1,000 years earlier.[1] We don't have a single 'grid' for history; we construct it when we want to resolve certain problems about who we are now.[2] We use narratives to define a subject – a person, a country, a process or practice – as something that exists and persists through time.

Thus a recent book of popular history like Norman Davies's *The Isles* begins by challenging the assumption that we know what we're talking about when we try to write the history of 'Britain'. What exactly are we doing when we group together this particular cluster of offshore islands and tell a story whose emphasis and direction suggests that they 'naturally' belong together as a unit? We may be doing all sorts of things – but one of them is quite likely to be reinforcing a belief that the picture of England and its dependent neighbours that came fairly naturally to our grandparents or great-grandparents is the 'natural' way of looking at the past of this group of islands. Awkward and uncomfortable facts are tamed or ignored, others are placed centre stage, often in ways that would greatly have surprised some of the people originally involved.[3]

This is not to be captured by fashionable doubts about 'objective' history or the sort of ultra-scepticism about the historian's bias which makes it almost impossible to trust any narrative. It isn't that narratives are false or wrong, simply that it helps to know some of the questions they think they're answering (or are answering without realising that's what they are doing). And I return here to my opening point: when you sense that you cannot take for granted that things are the same, you begin to write history, to organise the collective memory so that breaches may be mended and identities displayed. A French philosopher[4] has proposed that 'History (in the modern sense of the word) and revolution are born together'; meaning, I take it, that when there is a major rupture in the corporate experience, people cannot avoid seeing their past as strange in some ways. Making sense of that strangeness and arguing a case for or against the new foundations that have been laid in the revolutionary experience go together and, for this writer as for some others, set the agenda for the 'modern mentality' ('conservative' as much as 'progressive').

The point is a good one in helping us see something of the problems of that modern mentality (and we shall be looking again at some of its implications). But, while the application to the modern period is clear enough, there is a case for saying that the underlying question goes back to the very origins of Christian language, even if the full implications did not surface until the nineteenth century. To quote another French writer, a theologian this time, 'Christianity is not one of the great things of history; history is one of the great things of Christianity.'[5]

Even more accurately, perhaps, we could say that the work which the Bible does itself lays some of the essential foundations for history. The Jewish people tell their story in the light of a whole series of disruptions – the exodus, the coming of the monarchy, the division of the monarchy, the exile. Some recent scholars[6] have gone so far as to say that the Hebrew Scriptures are practically a historical novel designed to give a pedigree to a quite rootless group of settlers in what came to be Judaea, people who had been relocated there by the Babylonian administration. And while this is a wildly unlikely thesis as an account of the foundation in actual corporate memory for the Old Testament narrative, it does at least remind us that the narrative is trying to make a coherent picture out of a history of immense disruption, failure and displacement.

For the writers of the New Testament, the same is true in even more dramatic terms. By the time the first texts in the New Testament were being written, Christians were aware of tensions over whether they still shared the same identity as Jews; there were no short answers (there still aren't in some important respects). There was, they believed, fulfilment; there was also redefinition. And while these texts were being written and developed and responded to, the dramatic events which marked the end of Jewish political independence (the fall of Jerusalem in 70 CE) added a further element in Christian interpretation, with some long and unhappy consequences.

Thus what we read in the New Testament is not a simple record of what happened, but also a hugely creative and innovative attempt to make one story out of a set of memories that covers events of great disruptive force. Jesus brings the earlier history to a climax, yet in such a way that the history is seen quite differently; what matters in the earlier story will be different depending on the point of view of the telling, and passages and incidents that did not necessarily occupy the foreground now take on fresh significance. This, incidentally, is why Jewish–Christian dialogue can be very complicated: the Christian will read Hebrew Scripture looking for answers to questions that the Jewish reader isn't asking. But the point is that the New Testament writers know quite well that they have to present a story that is both coherent in essential ways and yet does justice to the novelty of what happens in the life and death of Jesus. They cannot unequivocally say either yes or no to the history of God's people as the Hebrew Scripture they were reading sets it out.

In this, they are doing nothing that is not already happening in the Old Testament itself, which goes on rewriting its own history. Look, for example, at Hosea 1:4, where the massacre of Jezreel, implicitly celebrated elsewhere as the triumph of orthodox faith over idolatry, is roundly condemned. Because God works in a long and varied historical process, the perspective within the Hebrew Scriptures is necessarily one that is constantly developing and moving; if Jesus is the culmination of that process, his life and death will provoke an unprecedentedly far-reaching shift of perspective, and thus a major essay in historical revision.

The New Testament sets out to show that Jesus' story is the

key to all other stories of God's dealings with his people, despite the discontinuities, the newness of what has happened through him. It also has to display a unity *within* the life of Jesus and the life of the early Church. It has to show that the Risen Jesus is the one who was crucified, that the faith of the early community is rooted in the words and events of Jesus' ministry, that the immense novelties of that community's life, as it gradually moved away from insistence on circumcision and food laws, represented a final and unsurpassable stage in the one story that began with Abraham and Moses. The first great essay in church history, the Acts of the Apostles, had to show that what was being preached at Rome in the 60s was part of a single organic movement beginning with the witness of the first apostles in Jerusalem. Nothing has changed; everything has changed. There is one story; there are enormous breaks and redirections. Read with imagination, the New Testament can be seen as a great attempt to write history in just the sense that our French philosopher intended – as a consequence of revolution.

And if I may refer briefly to a point that has been argued at greater length elsewhere,[7] all this gives us an important clue as to the kind of thing that most deeply worried the earliest Christians. Time and again, what they identified as heresy turns out to be, in one form or another, a system that reintroduces into a world rather precariously put together again after great ruptures some kind of deep division – between Old and New Testaments, between Christ and God, between the divine and the human natures of the Saviour. Christians are aware that, because of Jesus Christ, a familiar world has been broken apart and reassembled; so what becomes most frightening is anything that threatens to break up the universe again, driving wedges between what has been carefully stitched together by way of much paradox and skilful redefinition.

We shall be returning to all this in the second chapter; the point for now is that Christians from the beginning have a strong investment in history as a discipline which seeks to hold together in one story continuity and discontinuity. That is the

Why Study the Past?

nature of their story, with its unexpected fulfilments of prophecy, its crucified God. Christians are people (just like the Jews
after the exile) for whom the past has become a problem, a challenge, to be talked about, talked through, mended and unified in
language. The strange and interruptive has to be made into a
unity, has to be made intelligible, yet not reduced and made so
smooth that you don't notice there is a problem. The action of
God is allowed to appear in the telling of such a story as that
which holds together apparent contradictions and drives us to
deeper levels of consistency.

The temptations to short cuts were strong and serious. There
were those for whom the story was a drama in two acts – the
age of darkness represented by Hebrew Scripture, the enlightenment brought in Christ. There were those who went still further
and proposed that the Hebrew Scriptures were a sort of mirror
image of the truth, so that the evil characters who rebelled
against the stupid and malign God of the Old Testament were
really heroes and saints: the really important characters in
Genesis were the serpent and Cain.[8] But those whom we now
think of as mainstream Christians refused to give up so easily
and continued to maintain that the same God was at work in the
entire story; many early Christian confessions of faith explicitly
stress that there is one God inspiring the prophets, the apostles
and the community of contemporary believers.

In other words, history could, for the Christian, show the
faithful coherence of God's action and nature. Telling the story
of God's acts could display in dramatic form the consistency of
God's goodness. But because the human record is anything but
consistent, the historical enterprise is always going to have an
element of inviting *wonder* at the capacity of God to maintain
the steadiness of his work in the middle of earthly conflict and
disruption. Christian historical writing will always have something in common with what the Lutheran tradition has called
the theology of the cross: God can only fully show what it is for
him to be God by living through the abandonment of the cross,
through the apparent denial of his own purpose in tragedy and

hellish suffering. In that sense, the very difficulty of making sense, making a tidy and edifying story, becomes part of the theological point of the whole enterprise; the actuality of failure reinforces what is being said about God.

This is to go a lot further than the first Christian historians consciously intended. But the very effort to make any kind of historical narrative can be seen as a sort of act of faith, faith that massive disruption does not in fact destroy the possibilities of understanding, and thus the possibility of a shared world across gulfs of difference. It is a point we shall need to come back to — the idea of history itself as a moral or spiritual undertaking which gives us grounds for assuming it is possible to share a world with strangers. But this also helps us see why for a Christian the writing of history is bound to be theological in some ways. It is not that considerations of doctrine decide the results of research; God forbid. But the possibility of telling a consistent or coherent story about how God's people have lived is inescapably, for the believer, the possibility of seeing two fundamental theological points. God's self-consistency is to be relied on (i.e., God is not at the mercy of historical chance and change); and thus relation to God can be the foundation of a human community unrestricted by time or space, by language or cultural difference.

II

Writing history has to find a balance between concern with difference and concern with continuity. To make one story — especially on the far side of major upheavals, revolutions, which (as we have seen) some people think to be the primary place where history starts getting done — requires us to take the risk of supposing that thoughts and motivations don't change so fundamentally that we cannot imagine how people decided or hoped in earlier ages. But the figures the historian deals with are not modern people in fancy dress; they have to be listened to as they are, and not judged or dismissed — or claimed and enrolled as supporters – too rapidly. In one of the great historical quarrels of the nineteenth century, the Roman Catholic historian, Lord Acton, accused the Anglican scholar, Mandell Creighton, of being too indulgent in his judgements of the medieval and Renaissance popes. Acton wanted a more robust moral sentence passed; Creighton insisted on the need to allow some contextual elements into the judgements made on past ages. Creighton was in part arguing that the strangeness of a fifteenth-century mind had to be factored in to any interpretation, even a moral one; Acton's point is that this can be an excuse for relativism, and a betrayal of the moral purposes of writing history in the first place.[9] The quarrel is not one that can be easily resolved; it shows something of the tensions that arise when you recognise a moral dimension to the writing of history. But the point to bear in mind at this stage is that the risk of not acknowledging the strangeness of the past is as great as that of treating it as purely and simply a foreign country.

But it is time now to turn to some specific examples of the writing of church history which will illustrate the challenges of doing justice to both sameness and difference. After the first great enterprise of the Acts of the Apostles, we find little in the early Church that can be called systematic history writing. There are records of local events, especially martyrdoms, often included in letters to other local communities; there will be more to be said about these records in the second chapter of this study. But before the fourth century of our era, no one settled down to survey the whole. This was partly because, apart from these records of martyrdoms, the events of the Church's life were necessarily private; as a body treated by the Roman Empire as illegal, the Church becomes 'visible for record' primarily and almost exclusively when it comes into open conflict with the state. Its real history in the minds of its members is the biblical record; contemporary Christians, in those early centuries, saw themselves as living out the patterns defined by scriptural events, and when this story intersects with that of 'public life' in the Roman Empire, it is so that another episode may be added to the central story of God's kingdom in confrontation with the empires of this world.

Eusebius of Caesarea, at the beginning of the fourth century, is the first writer we can confidently call an historian in the usual sense among early Christian writers; and in the evolution of his work, we can see the mix of concerns that fed into the process, not least the different and persistent theological themes.[10] He probably wrote the first draft of his *Ecclesiastical History* before 300, at a time when the Church was emerging a little more into public visibility. Certainly, its doctrinal disputes had become more public (legal intervention had been sought to resolve the effects of at least one such debate), and this seems to have been one factor in Eusebius' decision to produce a more systematic chronicle than hitherto. He is aware that in doctrinal dispute it is of the greatest importance to be able to produce precedents – once again, to display continuities. A major part of his purpose is thus to give a sort of anthology of earlier sources and records of faithful witnesses to truth, so as to help the cause of orthodoxy in the present, as he says in the first chapter of his work. But he is also concerned – uncomfortably for the modern reader – with aspects of the controversy with Judaism. He needs to show not only the fulfilment of prophecy in the history of Jesus, but also how later events have confirmed God's judgement against the Jews. Theirs is a history which has, in effect, come to an end – or rather, Jewish history now exists only as a dimension of Christian history. He uses, as do many Christians, the rhetoric of Old Testament history itself against Judaism: Deuteronomy and the books associated with its theology and style (including the books of Kings and parts of Ezra and Nehemiah) present the history of the Jews as a repeated pattern of divine grace and human betrayal, and the Christian historian simply applies this to what is for him the last and greatest crisis of Jewish faith. The chosen people, in Eusebius' eyes, have betrayed their calling in the most dramatic way in rejecting Jesus, and so divine grace allows a climactic punishment by way of the destruction of the temple and the exile and humiliation of the people.

In itself, this is a triumphalism which the modern reader, as I've said, will rightly find impossible to read with any sympathetic identification. But it is important to try and see a little of why this rhetoric is a development from the earlier and rather simpler idea that the history which mattered was the biblical story as lived out by Christian believers, and how it provided a very significant resource for dealing with unexpected developments. The upheaval out of which the Church originally comes is 'normalised' into the patterns of biblical history through this strategy: God's people should know that rejection is punished and that God makes new beginnings. But also the transfer to Christians of the status of being God's people means that they now face the same risks and threats as the people of the first covenant. Their story too may be one of gift and rejection and punishment.

Eusebius began writing his history, as we have seen, at a time when the Church seemed to have settled down a bit in the Empire and become attractive and respectable in some degree. But within a very short time, the worst and most systematic persecution ever was launched, by the Emperor Diocletian. Eusebius, in making sense of this, is able to use just the same theological pattern as he finds in Jewish history, quoting the Lamentations of Jeremiah and Psalm 89. The new chosen people have sinned as did the old, and history thus repeats itself as God allows the heathen to punish them. And, in a way that brings together several of his central themes, he identifies this sin with inner strife in the Church, a strife that persisted even after persecution had begun. There is good evidence that Eusebius' hero, the great Alexandrian theologian Origen who had died some fifty years earlier, had been condemned or at least attacked in some of the churches of Asia Minor around the time that the persecution began, and that quarrels about his orthodoxy had gone on in the mines and the jails in which Christians from different localities were thrown together.[11]

But faithfulness under pressure in turn brings its own reward. The martyrs and confessors by their heroic witness made good the Church's failings, and the unprecedented horror of Diocletian's persecution gave way to the unprecedented benevolence of Constantine, showering favours on the Church. Eusebius' history ends with more than a hint of what he was to elaborate in later tributes to Constantine: it is as if the end of history has arrived. A new day dawns, the persecutors are punished; in Eusebius' joyful version of the story, 'the whole human race was set free' (X.2.1). The Church takes its proper foreordained place as the true centre of the world's life; and Eusebius was to write in another work of how the single rule of the Emperor on earth mirrored the way the universe was ruled by the one God through his divine Word.[42]

For Eusebius, the point of church history is not to trace a development within the Church, not even to understand the present in terms of the past. It is to show what it is that has kept the life of the Church continuously intact, and to show also how the pattern of God's action as set out in Scripture has been reproduced in the Church's story – with, as before, a climax, a final vindication. The Church is kept going by the succession of faithful teachers, which overlaps with (but doesn't completely coincide with) the succession of bishops in their chairs. Eusebius is, for some reason, a little sceptical of bishops as such, independent of their association with true teachers – a scepticism which comes out in his chapters on Origen, and which goes far to explain his initial support of the charismatic teacher Arius against his bishop in Alexandria. But it is also, and more deeply, kept going by the succession of martyrs: in every period when the Church is brought under judgement for its shortcomings by persecution, there will be those who trust God's fidelity sufficiently to give their lives for the faith and thus help to vindicate God's purpose in a time of darkness and distress. And when that time is over, when the Good King comes, fidelity is rewarded. The Church has not changed or developed, but the world has; it has at last come round to the truth by means of the monarch's conversion. In a way, there is nothing left to happen; as surely as in *1066 and All That*, history comes to a full stop.

The gloomy irony is that Eusebius chose to ignore almost completely the events that most shaped the course of the Church's life for the rest of the fourth century – the beginnings of the 'Arian Controversy'. Although he was himself involved in this, in ways that seem later to have embarrassed him, he evidently considered the controversy as a problem that was either solved or on the verge of being solved by benign royal intervention. By the beginning of the next century, no historian could possibly have so rosy a view of the Church's record or of the Emperor's involvement; imperial interference on the side of what came to be seen as the unorthodox party, even imperial reversion to paganism under Julian in 360, left many Christians far more sceptical about what a good thing it was to have imperial interest in the Church. As Robert Markus argued, in a ground-breaking book on how early Christians approached history,[13] St Augustine's attempt to make sense of the history of the Roman Empire in Christian terms practically turns Eusebius on his head: there will never be a final happy ending within human history; the Church continues its journey through the devastation of the human world, making what use it can of the good things in its environment but keeping its eyes firmly on God as the only ultimate goal worthy of human desire.

Augustine does not expect human progress to witness to the gospel; if there are instances where history appears to vindicate Christian virtue, well and good, but we must not be under any illusions. There is a sense in which history provides a sort of negative confirmation of what Christians say about human nature, in that we can easily see how Godless societies self-destruct because they can have no goals that are not ultimately selfish and so are always liable to break down in rivalry. But this simply reinforces the warning that there are no happy endings to be sought. The true ending is already here, in the lives of holy people in whom God exercises his royal power. Augustine and Eusebius agree on one thing at least, that the Church does not change; but Augustine does not expect the world to change either. To the end of time, there will always be two kinds of human love, human motivation, creating two kinds of society – the commonwealth of God, in which everything is done for the sake of God and the neighbour, and the commonwealth of this world, whose best hope is only to limit the excesses of competitive, acquisitive violence by artificial and external means.[14]

Augustine's austere vision was not universally shared, of course; the temptation remained strong to produce what Augustine clearly thought impossible – a history of Church and world which would be tidy and edifying. The true Church has no real history, since it is always that community of persons (not wholly coterminous with the membership of the visible institution, in which there will always be those not fully obedient to God) in whose lives the kingdom has come. There are stories to be told of how such persons came to their understanding of God; and Augustine, more than almost any other Christian thinker, gives full value to the centrality of change and growth in human selfhood. But if you find yourself narrating the story of the Church, the chances are that you will be telling a story of betrayal or decline: the visible Church appears as the distinctive subject of a story precisely to the degree that it is affected by the commonwealth of this world and is distracted from its task by the unconverted passions that flourish in the world. If the real Church does not change, a changing Church is in some measure unreal. And this may be a frustrating perspective if you are looking for stories that will in some way back up an argument in a current situation where there is sharp conflict. Augustine seems to leave little room for a church history that will serve polemic of one sort or another, a history that will prove points.

Yet when we turn to Bede, historian of the early English Church, we see how he can pick up something of the Augustinian vision and still produce a history that is quintessentially a point-proving exercise. Christians are capable of dramatic unfaithfulness, so that some local churches effectively become pseudo-churches. The true Church may have no history; but when it has to struggle to establish itself over against a 'failed' local church, there is indeed a story to be told. Bede's history is not simply about how the Anglo-Saxons became Christians, however much that innocent reading may once have prevailed. It is centred upon two themes. The first is more overt: it is the victory of Roman Christianity over what Bede sees as a corrupt local variation, the 'British' churches. Although technically neither heretical nor schismatic, they constitute a sort of counter-Church in their refusal to evangelise the Germanic settlers and to submit to the liturgical discipline of Rome. The second theme is implicit: the self-definition of the Germanic settlers as *a* people through their allegiance to Rome. The 'English' are essentially the coalition of convert Germanic kingdoms who have accepted the Roman mission.[15]

The rebellious pride of the British churches leads them to refuse to share the gospel with the settlers, thus denying them a part in the commonwealth of civilised peoples bound together by fellowship with the Roman see. The English become a distinctive nation, it seems, only when they become part of the Catholic commonwealth. It is proof of the sinfulness of the British that they not only hold aloof from full Catholic unity but deny it to others. *Their* history, for Bede, is a still starker version of Eusebius' revived Old Testament pattern: they have sinned and their kingdom is taken from them.[16] Those sins are already at work before the Germanic settlement; Bede is happy to use the fifth-century polemics of the British Gildas against his countrymen, though Gildas' purpose is nothing to do with relations with Rome.[17] British Christians invited the invasion by their sins and then filled up the measure of them by failing to evangelise and failing to co-operate with Rome's attempts to make up for their own dereliction.

This, then, is a confrontation between a church that could be said to have no history – the Roman church which is, in Eusebian style, the true centre of the world's life, a fixed point that does not change – and a church that has a history precisely because it has betrayed its calling. In the record of this confrontation, we may see how a nation is born, a community that from henceforth has some sort of separate identity – and which therefore will now be able to tell its own story as a real and distinct subject. Because it has received the gift of incorporation into Catholic fellowship, the 'English people' will from now on know who they are and possess a coherent historical tradition. The history of the Church (of the victory of the *true* Church, that is), in this context, is the basis for national history; and another element is added to the increasingly complex mixture of motivations for studying and relating church history.

Both Eusebius and Bede are wrestling with recent histories of acute conflict and disorientation. To risk a sweeping generalisation, the medieval period produced no ecclesiastical historians of quite their stature because the chroniclers of the period were seldom if ever dealing with crises of the same scale. Some comparable work is done through the medium of individual biography, when a charismatic figure has challenged the mainstream Church at a deep level and needs to be 'naturalised' into the ordinary and continuing story of the Church, as in the case of Francis of Assisi; but there is far less impulse to tell a larger story of crisis, interruption and recovery. Medievals simply had less to prove, on the whole. They produced chronicles, of course, and often (as in the theological controversies between East and West) dossiers of documents for argument.[18] But the study of these reinforces the perception that no one thought in terms of historical process, structurally or intellectually – which is why the theological debates between Byzantium and the West were so persistently deadlocked. It is not surprising, then, that the next great explosion in the writing of church history comes with the Reformation.

Reformation history reinstates the confrontation between true Church and pseudo-Church with a vengeance. For the Reformers, it is not that a local church has betrayed its calling and lost its integrity; the whole public apparatus of Christendom has become unrecognisable as a true church. The supreme authority of Christendom is in fact Antichrist. Martyrdom is inflicted not by a pagan state but by the pseudo-Church. If we think about the most popular historical work of the English Reformation, John Foxe's *Actes and Monuments* – Foxe's Book of Martyrs, as it is more generally known – we can see how the themes of both Eusebius and Bede are revived and incorporated in a radically new theology of church history. As in Eusebius, the history that matters is bound up with a succession of witnesses faithful unto death, and their suffering is vindicated by the arrival of godly government at last. As in Bede, the story is one of struggle between true and false Church, with the victory of the true Church heralding the birth of a nation under God, endowed with a providential calling. But here the true Church is persistently a persecuted minority *within* what pretends to be the Church; the elect nation realises its calling not by joining but by repudiating the commonwealth of nations allied to the see of Rome.

Recent scholarship has noted how the mere fact of suffering at the hands of Roman authority more or less suffices, in Foxe, for someone to be recognised as belonging to the true Church – with the result that he includes among his martyrs a good few who would have had an equally bad time under a mainstream Protestant regime, and rather glosses over the actual beliefs of some of these.[19] It is another ironic and unconscious reversal of Bede: just as affiliation with Rome is all you really need in Bede's world to be an acceptable spokesman of true Christian faith, and opposition, even of the most implicit and innocuous kind, disqualifies you, so opposition to Rome is all you need in Foxe's world to qualify you for membership in the true succession of witnesses.

So for the first time in the history of church history, the shape of the drama is one of primitive catastrophe, a devastating loss at or near the very beginning. There is a ghostly echo of those gnostic readings of the Old Testament in which there is a cosmic fall that makes all the supposed heroes of the story villains, and vice versa. The study of the past, remote and recent, is not

---

undertaken to show continuities, but to display a record of unremitting conflict in such a way as to render the existing situation in the present drastically open to question. Continuity alone no longer settles the issue; what matters is continuity with the party that maintains truth.

Protestant history, then, is never a simple repudiation of the Christian past, but what modern jargon would call a 'problematising' of it, a making strange.[20] We need to read our records with vastly increased care and discernment; we need to be able to recognise in early Christianity what has been forgotten or distorted later in the story. Hence the appeal of Reformed Christianity to the Fathers, and the new passion for studying and editing their works.[21] Protestant scholarship sought to present to its public and to its opponents a familiar tradition made strange and new. The often-quoted observation about the Reformation controversies as a confrontation between two aspects of St Augustine's theology (his doctrine of grace and his doctrine of the Church) draws attention to how Protestantism could excavate a new Augustine; but something similar can be seen in every Protestant anthology of texts from the Fathers.

What you thought was the 'real' story is no such thing; and the familiar must become unfamiliar in order to make this clear. In response, the defenders of Catholic tradition have just as much work to do: their task is to lay out the record in such fullness that it becomes impossible to identify a point of discontinuity or dissonance between then and now; and to deny any degree of dissonance within the record of the past that could justify appealing to one aspect or element in the theological tradition over others. The Fathers say the same thing, and say the same thing as we now say; there is no hidden alternative history.

Both strategies require a pretty encyclopedic treatment of the sources; so the sixteenth and seventeenth centuries are par excellence an age for the comprehensive assembling of sources, from the work of Cardinal Baronius and the Protestant compilers of the 'Centuries of Magdeburg' to Tillemont in the seventeenth century.[22] But a new element comes in with the explicit recognition that the continuity of belief itself needs justifying. Protestant radicals – especially in Italy and Poland – had turned their attention from debates over church order and sacramental theology and even sanctifying grace to raise a question as embarrassing for mainstream Protestants as for Catholics: if certain areas of theology have become unrecognisably corrupt and primitive truth has to be excavated laboriously from the ruins, how do we know that such corruption does not affect even the major themes of theology – the doctrine of the Trinity and the Incarnation? As more early Christian literary material became better known, there seemed more reason to ask this kind of question; and new levels of sophistication in interpretation were needed, by Protestants and Catholics alike, to combat these doubts.[23]

The seventeenth and early eighteenth centuries are also, therefore, an age for comprehensive documentation in regard to intellectual history. But methods and expectations vary. In France, in what was undoubtedly a golden age of patristic scholarship, the Jesuit Denis Petau (Petavius) took the bold line of stealing the radicals' clothes and thereby making a powerful point against mainstream Protestantism as well. Of course doctrinal formulae in the earliest Christian writers are ambiguous at best, sometimes plain wrong by later standards; this is because there was as yet no full recognition of the role of the Bishop of Rome as guardian of the faith. The woolliness of a second-century writer about the Son's equality with the Father does not throw into any doubt the truth of the Nicene Creed; but it does remind us that our trust in that Creed rests not on the authority of any ancient author but on the God-given powers of the Pope to confirm credal doctrine as true. Without this, the orthodox Calvinist has no convincing argument against the radical who wants to abandon infant baptism and trinitarian belief.[24]

Against this, other scholars fought energetically. Not all Catholic theologians were too happy with letting everything rest on the Pope's ratification; but some of the fullest responses came from Anglicans, determined to make out the historical case for continuity without invoking a referee. The Anglican Bishop Bull's work in defence of the Nicene Creed was applauded by Catholics as well as orthodox Protestants for establishing to the satisfaction of many that doctrinal consistency can be claimed throughout if we are careful to read ambiguous formulae with full attention to their context and to the possible range of meanings that words might have in such a context.[25] It is not, as is sometimes assumed, a pig-headed and unhistorical way of reading early texts; in some ways, by allowing for subtle nuances in usage and refusing to condemn simply on the basis of isolated formulae, it has advantages over both Petavius and the Unitarian radicals. It does, though, assume ultimately that everyone really *believed* the Nicene doctrine in the first three centuries, even if they didn't quite say so; and this begs a question or two.

Some of these matters will be coming up again later, and I shall have more to say about them. But the present point is that the Reformation generates a whole new set of attitudes to the Church's past. What is in front of you in the present moment needs arguing, justifying; it doesn't have to be this way. Even if you assert that it *should* be this way and really always has been if you know how to read the sources, you still have to work to make the case. And the powerful idea has been introduced that the past might be a source of deception; that there has been a primitive disaster in which truth has been lost or overlaid. From the very beginnings of church historical scholarship in Germany especially, this model had immense influence; it is not too much to call it a foundational myth of this tradition (irrespective of whether any particular bit of analysis in these terms is historically accurate). The greatest of eighteenth-century German church historians, Mosheim, set out at enormous length his understanding of an intellectual history which was early on captured by the alien forces of Platonic philosophy, so that authentic Christian thought was repeatedly distorted by the influence of this cuckoo in the nest.[26] And at the end of the nineteenth and the beginning of the twentieth century, Adolf von Harnack gave definitive shape to the myth, in the name not of Unitarianism or Pietism but of a liberal reconstruction of the gospel of Jesus which removed all strictly dogmatic content.[27]

Throughout the twentieth century this model continued to have immense influence. Bultmann was not a liberal in any proper sense of the word, but he still uses the basic structure of a primitive proclamation promptly corrupted into doctrine and 'Catholic' usage; generations of German and other New Testament scholars followed suit.[28] And most recently debates about the status of women in Christian tradition have some-times, consciously or not, worked with the same pattern. Elisabeth Schüssler Fiorenza's formidable work on Christian origins still envisages a sort of 'unfallen' early community in which egalitarian attitudes prevailed.[29]

Let me be clear: I am not in the least saying that such recon-structions are automatically wrong, should not be attempted, or are necessarily intellectually shabby. What is important is simply to recognise that they use a myth which is in many respects like any other myth, a framework for interpreting so familiar that it feels natural. To relate the story of the Christian Church is always – at least for the Christian – to look for a 'plot' in the record. It may be Eusebius' theme of suffering and vindication, Bede's tale of the battle between false and true versions of the Church, or the immense conspiracy theory of a certain kind of Reform-ation history, the Christian movement kidnapped almost from its beginnings by alien forces, so that a true identity has to be reconstructed laboriously from the doctored archives. But all this illustrates very clearly how much church history shares in what we have already recognised as one of the central motifs of all historical writing – the attempt to define the very subject whose history is being attempted. We begin with a sense of identity that is in some way fragile or questionable, and we embark on the enterprise of history to make it clearer and more secure. In the process, of course, definitions may change a good deal, but the aim is to emerge with some fuller sense of who we are.

Good historical writing, I suggest, is writing that constructs that sense of who we are by a real engagement with the strangeness of the past, that establishes my or our identity now as bound up with a whole range of things that are not easy for me or us, not obvious or native to the world we think we inhabit, yet which have to be recognised in their solid reality as both different from us and part of us. The end product is a sense of who we now are that is subtle enough to encompass the things we don't fully understand. Just as, in a good analysis of an individual self, we emerge with a heightened awareness of the strangeness within, so with history. We are set free from the crippling imprisonment of what we can grasp and take for granted, the ultimate trivialising of our identity.

So bad history is any kind of narrative that refuses this difficulty and enlargement – whether by giving us a version of the past that is just the present in fancy dress or by dismissing the past as a wholly foreign country whose language we shall never learn and which can only be seen as incomprehensible and almost comic in its savagery and ignorance. Both these sorts of narrative are very common at the moment. There have been some interesting arguments about historical drama on television and new broadcast versions of classical fiction: does the re-writing of dialogue and the 'modernising' of motivation, social custom and sexual behaviour serve to open up the past or to close it down, to make a classic more accessible or less? On the basis of what I have been arguing, the answer must be that its effect is to shrink the historical by ignoring or deliberately editing out what is strange, and so to leave us in our modern isolation. And this means that we have no way of understanding where and who we are because we do not allow our ways of being and thinking to be made strange to us by the serious contemplation of other ways of being and thinking.

Good history is irreducibly a moral affair – not quite in the way Lord Acton wanted it to be, perhaps (though judgement of behaviour, even in the past, is as inescapable as he asserted), but at the very least in persuading us to put some distance between ourselves and ourselves, between our imagination and what we habitually take for granted. Its effect may be radical or conservative: it may stir up in us a sense of real anxiety about what is at risk in the comfortable atmosphere of liberal modernity, it may expose the ways in which what seemed absolutely given and unarguable has prevented us from grasping that the way things are is the result of a process, not a natural law. History will not tell us then what to do, but will at least start us on the road to action of a different and more self-aware kind, action that is moral in a way it can't be if we have no points of reference beyond what we have come to take for granted. We return at last to the point with which this section began, the difficult balance between continuity and difference – the moral tension between respect for what is strange and freedom to interpret, address and argue with what is strange.

III

And of course on the basis of what has just been said about good and bad history, a great deal of the church history we have considered so far might be thought to be bad history: the impassioned search for justification in the past usually works by ignoring the differences between past and present. Eusebius quarrying for doctrinal continuities, even at what now seems a very brief distance from his sources, is still assuming that how people thought two centuries earlier is in no substantial way different from how they thought in his day. A Reformation theologian using a fourth-century source to show that contemporary Catholic thinking about the eucharist was a distortion of the real tradition took it for granted that the fourth-century writer was essentially dealing with the same questions, and could therefore give a yes or no to those questions. And for that matter, a contemporary arguing that primitive Christianity is fundamentally at one with modern feminism may be failing to reflect on how even apparently similar formulations or policies across the centuries may be drawing upon radically diverse sources. The primitive Christian may be and should be a source to use in questioning later tradition; but he or she does not cease to be a stranger. They are helpful to us not because they are just like us but in fancy dress, but because they are who they are in their own context.

That being said, the argument turns on its own tail. Eusebius and John Foxe wrote what we can't help seeing as bad twenty-first-century history – but they were not trying to write good twenty-first-century history. The strangeness of what they *were* trying to do poses a proper question to anyone looking at the history of history itself. The point is, of course, crucial in considering the vexed question of biblical historicity: it will not do either to suppose that biblical chroniclers had no recognisable sense of truthful narrative or to see them as (good or bad) modern narrators. Even the contemporary feminist reconstructing primitive theology and practice cannot simply be written off as a bad historian if what is being attempted is something other than ideological fiction; there is a somewhat different kind of enterprise being attempted in which canons of history-writing alone will not tell us everything. Once having identified these canons and recognised the dangers of making history answer our questions in our terms, we cannot go back to writing like Eusebius or Foxe, and we may have some quite proper questions to put to a Bultmann or a Schüssler Fiorenza at some points; but that is not going to be the end of the story.

In this last section, I want very briefly to explore what it might be that the standards I have specified do not tell us, and to suggest not only why church history is a moral matter but also why it becomes fully so only within a wider theological context. The Christian engaging with the past has even stronger reason for doing so as part of a maturation in critical and self-aware perception than the secular student, though there are important analogies even within the secular framework. A central aspect of where the Christian begins, the sense of identity that is there at the start of any storytelling enterprise, is the belief that the modern believer is involved with and in a community of believers extended in time and space, whose relation to each other is significantly more than just one of vague geographical

Why Study the Past?

connection and temporal succession. In theological shorthand, the modern believer sees herself or himself as a member of the Body of Christ.[30]

Who I am as a Christian is something which, in theological terms, I could only answer fully on the impossible supposition that I could see and grasp how all other Christian lives had shaped mine and, more specifically, shaped it towards the likeness of Christ. I don't and can't know the dimensions of this; but if I have read St Paul in 1 Corinthians carefully I should at least be thinking of my identity as a believer in terms of a whole immeasurable exchange of gifts, known and unknown, by which particular Christian lives are built up, an exchange no less vital and important for being frequently an exchange between living and dead. There are no hermetic seals between who I am as a Christian and the life of a believer in, say, twelfth-century Iraq – any more than between myself and a believer in twenty-first-century Congo, Arkansas or Vanuatu. I do not know, theologically speaking, where my *debts* begin and end. What any one believing life makes possible for others (and for which particular others) is not there for inspection. How my progress towards the specific and unique likeness of Christ that is my calling is assisted by any other Christian life is always going to be obscure.

I labour the point because it is in fact one that should on reflection look and feel difficult. We like to know our debts, we do not like to be moulded by forces, built up by contributions, that we cannot see and evaluate. Despite the popular postmodernist talk about how we are 'spoken by' language rather than speaking it, we worry about our boundaries; we do not like having them unpatrolled in the way that a robust theology of Christ's Body might suggest. But the truth is that, for anything resembling orthodox Christian belief, any believer's identity will be bound up with just this incalculable assortment of strangers and their various strangenesses.

Hence the Christian believer approaching the Christian past does so first in the consciousness that he or she is engaging with fellow participants in prayer and eucharist, fellow readers of the same Scriptures; people in whom the same *activity* is going on, the activity of sanctifying grace. This is not in itself the conclusion of research (they are so much like us that they must be the same really), but the implication of the Christian's basic belief that we are called into a fellowship held together not by human bonds but by association with Christ. Particular bits of historical research may make it harder or easier to put flesh on this fundamental conviction, but the only thing that could simply unseat it is a refusal of the underlying theology of the Church to which we are committed by practising the sacraments and reading the Bible. If you see Christianity simply as an enterprise of the human spirit within history, the challenge of understanding the past is going to be different, less radical. For the historian who has theological convictions, that challenge is to discern at last something of what is truly known of Christ in the agents of the past.

It will not do to have a simple progressivist myth which allows you to say that we know more of Christ than any earlier age; nor will it do to say that we have only to submit what we think we know of Christ to the judgement of our fathers and mothers in faith. It will not do to accept at face value what past sources have to say about themselves – there are indeed, as the feminist and the liberationist argue, suppressed voices to be attended to; but equally it will be inadequate to think of these suppressed voices as the only 'authentic' ones in the story. Church history, like all good history, invites us into a process of questioning and being questioned by the past; the difference is that the Christian past is unavoidably part of the Christian present in such a way that we have to be extra careful not to dismiss, caricature or give up the attempt to listen. What we are attending to is the record of encounter with God in Christ. How this affects our current thinking and decision-making is an issue to which we shall be returning more than once in what follows.

Eusebius and the others were right in this at least, that we need to approach the record in the expectation that what God has done God still does, that there is a sameness in the work of God which can only be fully understood as we trace the differences in the process by which one age leads into another. We are not the first to walk this way; run your hand down the wood and the grain is still the same. If all serious history drives us finally, as I think it does, to recognise that some sort of conversation is possible across surprisingly wide gaps in context and understanding, the same is true far more profoundly for the Christian, for whom such a conversation is the sign of belonging in one network of relations, organised around the pivotal relation with Jesus and his relation with God, into which Christians are inducted. Historical understanding is not a luxury in such a context.

But the labour of understanding is not made less by this. When we read the Bible, we do so, as Christians, in the belief that the God of Abraham is our God, and yet have to face the almost incalculable challenge of understanding Abraham as Abraham, not as a version of ourselves; a huge challenge because we do not know in what sense we can begin to see Abraham as a historical person, we do not know whether we see the shadow of a remote but real patriarch or simply the brilliant and God-directed literary creation of a personality by the storytellers of a later age. There is no short cut here that allows us just to speak of Abraham as one of us. But our faith will make little sense if we dismiss Abraham. Whatever tradition stands behind the stories we have, it is ineluctably part of what makes us who we are as believers, and we must expect as we labour with the text to find ourselves caught up in some kind of recognition. The inspiration of Scripture, as some modern writers have said, is not a matter of the Holy Spirit holding a writer's hand as a book is written; it is the *present* reality of a divine mediation that makes recognition possible as we now encounter the strangeness of the story. Abraham isn't 'one of us'; yet we and Abraham do make up an 'us' in relation to God, a shared reality before God which will take a lifetime to fathom.

So it is with the history of the Church. We are not dealing

with a holy text, but with the very untidy history of how the holy text has been read and lived out. But the same challenge is there: to be ready for recognition as we give full weight to what is strange. We are not allowed to come at this subject as if it were a series of displays behind glass. This is our world too. In the next two chapters of this book, I want to look in more depth at some of the issues around in the earliest days of Christian faith and then in the revolutionary epoch of the Reformation, asking how people in these settings worried about what the Church was and tried to find satisfactory models and definitions for it. My aim is to see if we can recognise in their worries things that are still worth worrying about; if we do find such recognition, we shall have found something of a common identity. We shall have begun to experience what it means to say that history is always trying to define its own object. Telling and hearing the story is itself a way of answering questions about what we're really talking about. Just as if we were writing a history of France or of medicine or of the papacy or of socialism, we shall discover a way of holding diverse things together in one narrative, we shall learn to evaluate why events matter in a particular way, and we shall end up thinking of our subject in a different way, having started by thinking we knew what it all meant and having found in the process of study that our definitions have to be stretched and remade by what is uncovered for us. But for the Christian involved in church history, the sense of recognition, of anxieties in common, becomes a reinforcement of belief in the Church itself as a society whose roots are in something more than historical process as usually understood. There will be in church history strong elements of institutional history, tracing the ins and outs of power games; there will be records of tragedy and betrayal; there will be long moments where we don't really know at all what made our ancestors work. As Christian students, though, we shall always be haunted by something else: to what call is all this a response – faithful, unfaithful, uncomprehending, transfiguring? Can we acknowledge it as our call too? And more to the point, can

we see that our immersion in the ways in which *they* responded becomes part of the way we actually hear the call ourselves
in more and more diverse and more and more complete
ways?

RESIDENT ALIENS:
THE IDENTITY OF
THE EARLY CHURCH

I

We know – surely? – what 'church' means; just as we know what 'science' means, or 'Britain' or 'German literature'. And, as I have been arguing in the first chapter, it is often only when we begin to try and construct a history of any of these things that we find how much we have been taking for granted and how little we can do to provide a timeless definition. The act of writing the history becomes itself a way of defining our subject. Part of that exercise is listening to the use of a word or group of words in a different historical setting: here is where some part of the story begins; what does this set of usages and conventions in language suggest about meaning and definition?

The world which the Christian gospel addressed certainly had no conception of anything much resembling 'church' as we use the word. The idea of a voluntary religious association, with local gatherings linked (in varying degrees of closeness) with similar gatherings elsewhere was one that had some limited ana-logues; the idea that these gatherings were constituted as a new version of the human race itself and that they made potentially exclusive claims to the loyalty of their members would have been very odd indeed. Civic Roman religion assumed that the true unit of sacred reality was the empire itself, with its public rituals and the unifying practice of venerating the divine power of the emperor.[1] Under this umbrella, international voluntary associations of a kind might flourish, though they were likely to be regarded without great enthusiasm by the administration.

There were groups practising specific rites of initiation into allegiance directed towards this or that deity of non-Roman origin – Mithras, Isis and Cybele, to take the best-known examples; such groups often had a professional priesthood very different from the civic priesthood of the imperial religion, and a focus upon individual enlightenment alien to imperial ritual. As such, they could provide an optional supplement to public religion, but not a substitute for it; the role of a professional clergy might raise anxieties about control and about the deleterious effects on families and family loyalty that might come from this 'clerical' element, but no one was liable to see this as a threat to public religion itself. The idea of *a* religion is alien in this context. There is simply the social order with its public rituals to guarantee stability and divine protection, with specific cultic practices arising here and there to offer more personal satisfaction. In the empire, the special case of Judaism was an exception proving the rule: here was a religious practice so inseparably tied to ethnic and social identity that it could not be treated as a private supplement to Roman public religion. But as a highly specific matter restricted to members of one race (and a not too worrying number of people who had ritually opted in), it could be more or less accommodated; it was not a rival in some competition for defining the universal context of human significance.

Christian groups were not quite like synagogues, nor were they quite like the optional devotional associations looking to exotic deities from abroad – though they had very obvious affinities with both, as the earliest records testify.[2] Their language about themselves was, however, strikingly different. There were at least three elements in this that would have caused puzzlement, especially when put together. In the texts they read to each other in their assemblies, Christians referred to themselves as *hagioi*, as people who were holy or sacred. They called the groups in which they met *ekklesiai*, 'civic assemblies'. And they also described themselves as *paroikoi* or *paroikountes*, 'resident aliens' or 'settled migrants'.[3] They claimed, in other words, that they occupied a distinctive place, the territory that belongs to the divine, that their corporate identity could be compared to a sanctuary; that they were 'citizens' of something; and that their actual roots and loyalties were in another context than the cities in which they actually resided.

A citizen of the empire encountering this sort of vocabulary and reflecting upon it would have been forced to conclude that Christians were identifying their sacred power as something connected with their status as somehow outsiders in the imperial structure. Reluctance to serve in the army or to accept civic office would have reinforced the point. These were people who saw their privileged access to sacred power and legitimacy as bound up with a deliberate and systematic distancing from the legitimate power of the sacred order of the empire; the claim to be both citizens (with the right to a civic assembly) and settled aliens could not but read as a statement of foreign allegiance, even if this was not allegiance to a specific foreign power. The language that defined 'church' was unmistakeably a language that raised problems for a system claiming to be the ultimate source of holy and legitimate power.

Against such a background, we may better understand why, for the first hundred years or so after the writing of the literature of the New Testament, the most distinctive genre of Christian writing is the narrative of martyrdom. The story of the Christian tried and executed by the imperial power is the most dramatic but also the simplest possible demonstration of what 'church' means – and so of what holy power looks like and what is involved in claiming a different sort of citizenship. Martyrdom is a demonstration of Christian 'legitimacy', of the foundational charter of that community which is called the *ekklesia*: this is what the rule and law of God means, and why the legitimacy of the empire cannot be the last word.

Examples are abundant. If we look at the second-century African document recording the deaths of a group of Christians at Scilli in Numidia in 180, a document almost wholly unadorned in its narrative, we can see exactly where the critical questions come.[4] The group, judging from their names, are mostly ethnic North Africans, possibly a mixture of house slaves and freedmen (some of them are taxpayers); they are not all that sophisticated or literate, with one or two exceptions. Initially, charged with Christian profession, they try to explain that they behave like ordinary citizens, paying their taxes, avoiding civil disturbances and praying divine protection for the emperor. But, the magistrate insists, this does not add up to real religion so long as they do not pay cultic honour to the emperor's divine power. The accused respond with what is obviously a reference to Jesus' 'Give Caesar what is Caesar's and God what is God's' – distinguishing the worship owed to God alone, who is king over all kings, from the purely 'secular' respect and loyalty owed to the emperor. They decline to take the time offered to think it over and are summarily condemned; they greet the sentence with thanksgiving.

It is a moving story, not least because of the monosyllabic simplicity of the martyrs; and it eloquently sets out exactly where the collision between the empire and the civic assembly of settled migrants, the citizens' meeting for non-citizens, most clearly arose. There is an appeal from the emperor's court – not in any worldly sense; the condemned are executed. But the legitimacy of the verdict is simply put in question by the claim that the imperial power is subordinate to another king and cannot therefore ask for unquestioning loyalty. This is the negative side of the Church's claim; there is also, though, a positive side, to do with the idea of the Church as locus of sacred power, which comes across more clearly in other documents, nowhere more dramatically than in the account of the martyrdom of Polycarp, Bishop of Smyrna, in (probably) 156.[5] Like the Scillitan narrative, it is contemporary with the events it portrays, though the literary elaboration of the telling is greater. Polycarp, urged to forswear Christ, replies, 'I have served him for eighty-six years and he has done me no wrong. How shall I abandon my king who has saved me?' It is the identification of Christ as king, here as with the Scillitan martyrs, that makes the point that the jurisdiction of the court before which he stands is itself under question.

But there is more. Polycarp is tied to the stake in the arena to be burned alive and utters a distinctively worded prayer as this is done, a prayer which is almost certainly intended to echo the kind of prayer he would have used at the eucharist. Whether or not he prayed in precisely these words is beside the point – though there is nothing unlikely about his having done so. Ignatius of Antioch, half a century earlier, who had corresponded with Polycarp in the latter's youth, had spoken of being ground by the teeth of the wild beasts in the arena as if to become eucharistic bread.[6] What matters is that Polycarp or his chronicler or both saw the event of his martyrdom as analogous to the sacrament. The parallel is reinforced by the detail that, when the fire is lit, Polycarp's body is seen as if it is bread in an oven, and a sweet smell pervades the theatre. The martyr consecrates his body to be a holy place exactly as the bread and wine of the eucharist become the place where sacred presence and power are to be found. The expulsion of the Christian from the would-be sacred order of the Roman city or the Roman empire is the very moment in which the holiness of the Christian is perfected: holiness, in the sense not of exceptional goodness but of the active presence of a holy and terrifying power, is indeed identical with marginality in the terms of the empire. The holy place is the suffering body expelled from the body politic, Polycarp uttering his great thanksgiving as the flames are lit.

The martyr stories often try (as does the account of Polycarp's death) to make this holy power somehow visible or tangible: swords are blunted, animals are cowed, executioners bungle their work, there is an effusion of blood that quenches the fire (as in Polycarp's case); the divine presence does not rescue the martyr but makes itself felt. Legendary as this may be, it simply underlines what is thought to be happening. The relating of the stories of the martyrs in this early literature, up to the mid third century, is an essential part of the Church's self-identification, part of the definition of the vocabulary of being an *ekklesia* of aliens, the citizens' assembly of the non-citizens, a people whose political legitimacy and loyalty lay outside the imperial system.

Why Study the Past?

It is noteworthy that the earliest martyr narratives, usually letters from one local church to another, regularly begin with the formula, 'The *ekklesia* of God living as resident aliens in X to the *ekklesia* of God living as resident aliens in Y'; the narrative that follows can be read as an explication of these introductory formulae.[7]

The second-century text called the *Letter to Diognetus* spells it out more prosaically in describing Christians as a foreign group living in the cities of the empire (and elsewhere, 'spread throughout the world'), distinguished by no special ethnic costume or alien language but by their allegiance and their consequent behaviour, at home everywhere and nowhere.[8] But the point we ought to take very seriously in all this is less the refusal to be identified with localised human power than the very demanding and specific conditions for being an expression of divine power. Christians behave differently – a frequent theme in second-century literature; they forswear promiscuity, infanticide (including abortion), fraud and violence; and of course, in the most public counter-cultural witness of all, they will face death for their commitment. This is not just a claim for moral superiority; some of what is boasted of would have been admirable to a Mediterranean citizen of high principle, some would have been incomprehensible. More important is the role such descriptions have of defining the separate identity of the *ekklesia*. And this makes sense of the concern – difficult and unsympathetic to many modern students – with the discipline and purity of the Church in the second and third centuries.

A certain sort of Protestant church history is liable to express disappointment that the gospel of free grace and absolution for sinners had degenerated by the early second century into a legalistic system calculating which sins committed after baptism, if any, could be formally remitted, what tariffs should be in place for particular misdemeanours and so on. When in the late second century one Bishop of Rome attempted to ease the official line on post-baptismal adultery, storms of protest resulted, with some very *ad hominem* polemic on the subject from one of the leading

Roman theologians of the day.[9] We are tempted to say, 'Pharisaism', and deplore it all. But this is to miss the point quite substantially. The specific and even measurable differences in Christian behaviour were a sign of the presence of divine power: up to the fourth century at least, the high standard of sexual continence evident in Christian communities was put forward as an argument for a unique level of divine assistance given to believers.[10] Compromise over adultery or abortion weakened such an argument and weakened the reality to which the argument pointed; the spiritual integrity of the community as a sacred place was under threat. And of course the sort of compromise involved in apostasy during persecution was for many an irreparable wound in the body. Through such wounds, power leaks away.

The persecutions of the third and early fourth centuries provided relatively easy opportunities for compromise because they were in significant measure designed as much to embarrass and confuse the Christian community as to exterminate it. In the mid third-century persecution of the emperor Decius, you had to obtain a certificate stating that you had sacrificed or offered incense as the courts required if you were to avoid prosecution as a Christian. Such certificates survive, with names and dates and witnesses.[11] It was possible to obtain a false certificate if you wished to avoid prosecution but also to keep your conscience clean. In the period after persecution had ceased or eased, the Church's leadership had to make some difficult decisions as to whether someone who had obtained a false certificate was to be treated as an apostate, and whether they and those who had actually taken part in a Roman civic ritual should ever be readmitted to the communion of the Church.

We tend to see this as an issue about rigorism over behaviour; but we need to acknowledge the deeper and more elusive motivations that had to do with fears about the loss of the Church's sacredness. The holy body, like Polycarp's body in the arena at Smyrna, must be one that is consumed by the divine; when other links and loyalties are at work, you cannot intelligibly argue about how the Church is really an assembly of the citizens of heaven and holy in virtue of its repudiation or relativising of other kinds of citizenship. And it is easy to see why the case of a bishop who had compromised in time of persecution, even of a bishop who was innocent himself but lenient to others, focused these anxieties most acutely. The bishop as president of the sacramental assembly was the one around whom the community found its visible unity at worship, in the eucharistic celebration where the body of believers, through identification with Christ's prayer to the Father, entered the heavenly sanctuary with the angels, received from Christ the miraculous food of immortal life and re-emerged newly constituted as the locus in the world of divine life and agency, a holy body. A failing or unfaithful bishop made nonsense of all this.

These were the matters that caused the deepest internal divisions within the Church prior to the fourth century. They illustrate what the language of the Church as a holy assembly of aliens came to mean in practice, and why martyrdom remained a touchstone of the Church's integrity. The celebration of martyrdom – and the claims of certain groups in times of controversy to be the *true* heir to the Church of the martyrs, as opposed to a corrupted hierarchy – is neither a cult of suffering for its own sake (not that there are no signs of obsessive interest in torture and physical extremity in some of the literature) nor an affirmation of the importance of dying for your conscientiously held beliefs. The martyr is the conduit of divine presence who vindicates the claim to another citizenship.

We understand very little about the early Church if we ignore this extremely concrete conception of where divine power resides. And equally, this casts light on the growing interest of Christians in virginity: particularly when martyrdom has ceased to be common (though there are instances before this), the virginal body becomes an analogue of the martyred body; consumed by God and unviolated by humanity, it is a localised channel of power. To read this – as moderns typically do – as no more than a negative attitude to sexuality is to miss the intimate connections between various kinds of refusal and distancing on the part of early Christians and their conviction of difference over against the sacred power of the state.[12] Christian or para-Christian theologies and practices that offer justifications for avoiding martyrdom, or that replace this theology of virginity with a generalised attack on marriage or the body, or that take the opposite extreme and reconnect the body's ecstasy itself with the sacred, are seen as abominations: the cluster of systems known collectively as *gnosis*, saving knowledge, included variations on all these themes, and they were all violently repudiated by writers of what became the mainstream.

It is out of this matrix that debates about doctrine arise. Once again, we misunderstand the early Church if we suppose that these debates were fuelled by a general concern for verbal precision or by intellectual interests alone. The controversies about Christ in the fourth and fifth centuries are in their own way debates about what it is to be citizens of that city whose supreme court is that of the Divine Word, what it is to claim that the ultimate legitimacy and coherence for human life together lies in Christ and that human history converges upon him; they are also about how sacred power is conveyed through him to the body of believers. Doctrine, in this environment, is profoundly to do with the actual possibilities of the 'alien citizenship' we have been examining.

II

Mention has been made of the systems of *gnosis*: they are very diverse in character, and it is a mistake to lump them together as something called 'gnosticism', but one or two themes recur regularly in the literature associated with them. One of the most frequent is the notion, mentioned in the first chapter, that revelation divides history in two, so that what happens before the Redeemer's coming is darkness and deceit. The visible world whose story we are told from creation onwards in the Hebrew Scriptures is the realm of untruth, manipulation by ignorant or evil powers; the knowledge given by grace through

Jesus provides the key to read what has hitherto baffled or deluded us.[13]

Now this undoubtedly reflects a real element in Christian discourse – the sense that what has happened in the events around Jesus has had the effect of radically reordering perception, radically altering the shape of the story of how God works. The gnostic version is one in which the rupture is complete: there is no way of establishing continuity with what has gone before except by treating it as a mirror image of the truth about the universe. But the element of discontinuity is not to be argued away easily. The world has been broken apart by the coming of Christ, his death and resurrection, and this is in part what grounds precisely that conviction about 'alien citizenship' which we have been considering. Both mainstream Christians and gnostics used language about believers as a different 'race' from others; some gnostics referred to themselves as the 'kingless race'.[14]

But the Christianity that emerged as the predominant voice was consistently anxious to put Humpty-Dumpty together again, as we might say; they wanted to re-establish a vision of the universe and its history that made one story, one system. Hence their strenuous opposition to any scheme that divided God the creator from God the redeemer and, increasingly, their opposition also to theologies that divided the human and the divine in Jesus.[15] There is a connection between what is said about the work and person of Jesus and what is being argued as the essence of the Church as a social reality. The Church is nothing if it is not an assembly of migrants, answerable finally to the law of another city: Christ must be unequivocally Lord and master of his circumstances, unequivocally the carrier of divine power, his own tangible person a sacred place. But the Church is also vulnerable to other powers as it lives in the world of matter and history; it must inhabit this world, because this is the world in which God has to vindicate his sovereignty. And so Christ must genuinely share the human condition, and his sufferings must be real. Weaken any part of this carefully balanced network of convictions and the rationale for Polycarp's witness and triumph in the arena slips away.

How we become holy in association with Jesus was thus the most practical of questions, so that the nature of Jesus' holiness was no academic issue. Hence the distinctive character of so much early Christian argumentation: it is not a simple and steady advance towards doctrinal purity and conceptual completeness, but an attempt to balance a number of potentially highly paradoxical concerns in the least unstable or nonsensical way, *in the light of specific practices of worship and corporate behaviour.* By the fourth century, writers are more than ever aware that a doctrinal programme devoted to exhaustive description of what it is like to be God is doomed; the only proper aim is to provide a language for speaking of God which is congruent with worship and what is recognised as human sanctity. And in case anyone wonders where the authority of the Bible enters in to this picture, it should be said that the Bible is central to the action of worship and to the provision of criteria for holiness – but that it is not abstracted from these functions as simply a bare text of reference.[16]

The history of doctrinal development could be described as a record of discarded solutions. Typically, a promising theory is advanced, explored, found wanting and left behind, with a legacy of terminological clarification and complexification to make the next round of discussion still more difficult. The definitions of the fourth and fifth centuries are not very stable compounds of these terminological experiments: a precariously balanced set of warnings and prescriptions, within whose boundaries we may expect to encounter the truth. To criticise them as unnecessarily elaborate philosophical theses is to miss their character entirely. The processes of debate give the terms their meaning, not some imagined philosophical hinterland; and they seek not to exhaust but to mark out where the risks and incoherences lie in talk about God's revelation.

Frequently, as is often remarked, they react against a too tightly worked theory which leaves out of account some

Why Study the Past?

fundamental concern. Thus the popularity in the first and second Christian centuries of theologies that played down the humanity of Jesus left out the significance of the human *locus* of his divine activity. If sacred power is not alive and sustaining itself in the midst of actual human suffering, something essential is lost. And if Jesus is the earthly form of some great angelic power – manifestly a popular structure within which to interpret him in the first Christian generations – this fits neatly (though in slightly different ways) into the cosmology of both Greek and Jewish belief, but leaves open the question of whether it is *God's* power we are dealing with. Rabbinic controversies over the existence of a 'second power' in heaven reveal that these issues were not unique to Christians.[17] Yet a theology that treated Jesus as a great human saint promoted to quasi-divine status for his achievement is – curiously to modern eyes – hardly in evidence at all. Even where the language of 'promotion' or exaltation is used (as in Acts or Hebrews in the New Testament), it is made clear that direct divine power is from the first at work in him and that the divine initiative is prior to any kind of reward for human virtue. When the most careful and sophisticated theory of all to date is advanced at the beginning of the fourth century by the Alexandrian priest Arius – a theory scrupulously grounded in liturgical language as well as terminological analysis – it provokes the most violent reactions to date.[18]

Arius' theory is probably the best attempt that could have been made to settle the issue of Jesus' holiness without some basic revision of the very meaning of the word 'God'. It proposed that the eternal Word embodied in Jesus was the primary recipient of God's revelation and God's glory and power, but also the primary worshipper of God – the revealer of divine truth but also the paradigm for the relation of creation to God. The fourth-century doctrinal crisis is a long and laboured effort to clarify what this leaves out, and it results in a redefinition of divine unity which is embedded in the creeds of historic Christendom. The details need not concern us just now. But in the light of the arguments made earlier in this chapter, it is very important to realise that one reason for suspecting Arius' solution was the infinite gulf left between God and the Word, so that the Word was still a reality contained within the universe. And if so, could the Word truly be the ground for a *wholly* different citizenship? Eusebius of Caesarea, whom we have met before, was a cautious supporter of Arius at first; and his own theology entailed a hierarchical picture of the universe in which divine power 'cascaded' from God to the Word and from the Word to the Christian emperor. Arius' opponents, frequently locked in controversy with a Christian emperor whom they believed to be doctrinally mistaken, were grateful for a theology that could *oppose* the Word to the emperor when necessary; for them, what we might call the Polycarp test was what made Arius and his supporters dangerous, absorbing the radical difference of Christ back into the systems of the created world. It is not accidental that Arius' opponents were much better represented among the monastic communities than his supporters; these were communities self-consciously standing in the tradition of martyrs and virgin ascetics of an earlier age.

Theology must justify the witness of the martyr; but in so doing it must also justify the belief that what is revealed and promised in the Christian gospel is the transfiguration of this world, the restoration of humanity to its proper place in a universe held together by *logos*, order or rationality, and held together *in* the Logos, the eternal Word of God. Hence, as I have said, the concern not to inscribe disruption at the heart of the Christian story. But in the fourth and fifth centuries, the focus shifts from the earlier concern to show that the gospel is continuous with Jewish history to the more exacting set of intellectual anxieties that centres upon the unity of divine and human agency in Jesus. The repeated accusation against unorthodox teachers from the end of the third century onwards is that they teach 'two Christs' – i.e., that they (like some gnostic writers) allow for some degree of separation between the divine person who acts in Jesus and the concrete human particularity of Jesus: a Christ 'from above' and a Christ 'from below'. And once again, this is a directly practical concern, in that what is said about Jesus immediately affects what is said about the eucharist and the nature of the divine presence and power in the consecrated bread and wine. Divorce the humanity of Jesus from the divine agency and the eucharist becomes – so some writers argue – either a mere memorial or communion in the flesh of a human being.

These are the factors that lead eventually to the most elaborate of the early Christian doctrinal settlements, at the Council of Chalcedon in 451. The eternal Word is God in the same sense as God the Father is God – as had been established by the Council of Nicaea in 325; but in Jesus Christ the eternal Word becomes the animating, defining principle of an individual human life, in such a way that you cannot separate the reality of this human life in anyway or in any moment from the underlying active life of the Word. There is one *hypostasis* involved, that is, one actively existing principle, eternally real in the life of the Trinity, becoming real in our world at the point of Jesus' conception. But this does not mean that the Word turns into something less than God, or that the human individual Jesus becomes other than human: the lesser reality is activated and transfigured by the greater, but not changed in essence.[19]

Around this formulation there developed a set of consequential problems to do with the nature of Jesus' human freedom, the sense in which he shared the 'corruptibility' of fallen human physicality, and other matters. But it is helpful to look sideways, as it were, at the way in which people were reflecting at the time on the life of prayer and asceticism. The monastic literature of the fourth and early fifth centuries develops the pattern of a contemplative ascent through the moral life to the perception of reason and order in creation and thence to that openness to God as God which evades all conceptual definition and is true *theologia*.[20] In other words, the person who prays is the person who both in behaviour and in understanding restores order to a disordered world, a person who makes visible the effect of submission to *logos*; he or she is someone who vindicates the Christian faith as a scheme that unifies the world of experience rather than fragmenting it. And the climax of the process is an acknowledgement of the absolute difference of God: holiness is both living in an ordered universe and recognising that this order is derivative from a reality quite uncontainable within it. It is as if the contemplative acts out in his or her life of prayer the relation between Christ's human and divine natures. The mature life of contemplation is an embodiment of *logos* (just as it might have been for a certain kind of philosopher), but that *logos* emanates from a reality that cannot be encompassed by rational perception, only by love and radical detachment and the silencing of analytical and imaginative activity. Just as in Christ, a human life is transfigured from within in function of an indwelling divine agency which is in loving relation with an infinite source. In and with Christ, the believer represents both the unshakeable order of the universe and the utter freedom and mystery of the self-giving God.

This is some way from the witness of Polycarp in the arena; but it continues to show signs of the same concerns. What is involved in the claim to be a place in the world – whether as individual or as community – in which sacred power is active to such a degree that it puts in question all local human claims to a final legitimacy and authority? Reflection on the apparently abstruse details of doctrine about the relation of Christ to God the Father or about the balance of divine and human in Jesus is a part of expounding what is meant by identifying the Christian *ekklesia* as both an assembly for those who are not at home in the present order and a revelation of true order – as a sign both of disruption and of harmony. The rather abstract accounts of holiness in the monastic literature I have referred to belong in just the same frame of discourse; and the persistent significance of the eucharist in all these discussions reminds us of where the *ekklesia* expressed its identity, its citizenship, most visibly.

Reading the history of the early Church in this perspective is one way of understanding what were the persistent concerns that gave unity to the diverse social phenomena that composed 'the early Church', what were the 'continuities of conflict', to borrow Alasdair MacIntyre's phrase. Doctrine is to be understood in the context of social facts, indisputably; but that is far from being a necessarily reductionist observation. There may be some for whom such an axiom means that doctrine is always an ideological story concealing the imposed structures of social power; and it would be a foolish historian who neglected the ideological elements in the record, the ways in which – not least in the fourth century – versions of history are already being constructed so as to justify or legitimise the position of the winners. It is not only the 'orthodox' who do this, incidentally; there are historians who reject the creed of Nicaea and who are just as capable of tailoring their records to their interests.[21] But what matters more, I believe, is the way in which the entire history draws upon a more basic set of social facts and relations – the very existence of the Church as what I have called an 'alien citizenship', refusing assimilation into the imperial city or state. This is something which the actual vocabulary of the first generations makes inescapable as a theme; I have been trying to show that it is a theme which still dominates and shapes doctrinal discussion even after the collision of *ekklesia* and empire has been radically changed by the ending of persecution. Despite the best efforts of some (like Eusebius, as we noted in the first chapter), it proved impossible to conclude that history had come to an end with the end of persecution; the question of spiritual authority, the distinctiveness of the revealed gift which the Church embodied, would not be muted, even in an environment where earthly power appeared as an increasingly tempting ally for the Church.

It was, of course, an ally to whose seductions the Church regularly yielded. What is striking about the history, though, is that, because the early concern about making sense of the witness of a Polycarp persisted through the various metamorphoses we have been tracing, the Church's doctrinal settlement continued to encode elements of *un*settlement; the doctrinal language which prevailed insisted on anchoring the Church's particularity firmly in a divine action. We shall be looking at some of the longer-term consequences of that in the next chapter; but for now the important point is that the Church left itself with an agenda, a set of questions about the relation of the *ekklesia* to the changing forms of political life. It left itself, we might say, with a rationale for thinking about history.

It may seem that the superficially obsessive interest in the Church's purity in the first couple of centuries, followed by an equally obsessive interest in doctrinal correctness together suggest a body eager to escape from the changes and vicissitudes of history. As usual, this sceptical perception is not to be glibly dismissed. We have seen in the first chapter how very readily the Church's chroniclers and apologists turn to a model of the Church's continuity that claims unchanging sameness. But the fact is that the agenda set by the question of the Church's distinctiveness and legitimacy produced a steady process of rethinking and clarifying, both of discipline and of doctrine; it gave the Church work to do which was never simply repetition. The obligation to display continuity or coherence in changing circumstances led to that continual retelling which we began by examining in the first chapter. We understandably look with caution at claims to unchanging correctness; but we should not for that reason underestimate the importance of the intellectual creativity that went into shaping and reshaping a history with some claim to intelligible unity.

The very fact that concerns which in the second century generated controversies about the limits of acceptable behaviour in the Church had by the fourth century begun to generate new issues about cosmology is significant. And in this context also, the earlier concerns about purity and integrity in the Church's life do not disappear but are worked into a more sophisticated theology. The somewhat cynical commentator might observe that it is simply a more realistic theology, accommodating the lower standards inevitably consequent on larger numbers and looser control; but there is a theoretical argument as well. In his disputes with rigorist opponents – the Donatist congregations of

North Africa who held that misconduct by a bishop invalidated all his sacramental actions and contaminated all who communicated with him or were ordained by him – Augustine of Hippo contended strongly against a picture of the Church's purity or legitimacy that depended on an unbroken pattern of lawful behaviour and nothing else.[22] What distinguished the Church, what gave it its theological identity, was not, he maintained, the fact of consistent repudiation of sin, but the fact of consistent acknowledgement of sin and the daily prayer for forgiveness.

Augustine's critics held that the past apostasy of bishops invalidated the entire life of the churches they had led – a view with clearly visible roots in earlier discipline. But Augustine famously notes that the prayer most frequently prayed by Christians at the command of their Lord includes a petition to be forgiven their trespasses: are we then to pit our perfectionism against the realism of Jesus? Growth in the life of the Church is growth in *caritas*, love enabled by the gift of the Holy Spirit through the community's life and sacramental practice.[23] If it is seen in terms of the excellence of individual moral attainment, a consistently clean slate in respect of grave and public sin, does this not open the door to pride and thus close the door to that humility which alone is the condition for letting Christ enter? Holy power becomes available through humility, and thus through the constant identification and owning of sin.[24] So 'purity' is not to be defined in the language of achievement or of avoidance but of single-minded self-exposure to God's pure truth. As in his account of the Church's relation with the history of worldly power, Augustine does not look in this world for a static resolution beyond which lies no change for the better. The concern is the same: what makes the Church holy? The answer is subtly but substantially different. The holiness of the indwelling Spirit who causes Christ to be alive in us comes into us through a radical putting aside of self-reliance. We must learn to tell our own stories as believers in the mode of recognition of our weakness and witness to God's power to restore – *confessio*, acknowledgement, in the double sense of admitting failure and pointing to where help is to be had. There is a clear line joining Augustine's autobiographical 'confessions' and his attacks on Donatism.[25]

What we see here, I suggest, is the beginning of a movement that will bear fruit in the Reformation era in some very clear ways. It is the move away from defining the integrity of the Church in terms of its visible achievements or the unbroken consistency of its practice and towards a definition in relation to the action of God within it. It represents in one way a weakening of the second-century conviction that consistent holy behaviour was simply a mark of God's presence; it dug a ditch between feeble human effort and divine involvement which could be seen, and by some was seen, as collusion with sinfulness and passivity (hence the attacks on Augustine not only by the ascetic Pelagius but by a good many who took for granted a more integrated picture of how divine energy and human decision and habit worked together). It threatened in new ways the precarious reassembling of a harmonious universe to which Christian theology was committed. Yet it challenged in the most radical way possible any account of the Church's unity that made it depend on contingent and historical factors. Augustine is unmistakeably working with the real questions of an earlier period, but implying that their fully theological resolution will need some new and disturbing turns in the argument; and in that sense he is doing something very like the prelates at the Council of Nicaea who reluctantly adopted a fresh terminology in order to hold on intelligibly to a threatened belief.

III

The issues of the Church's distinctiveness and the Church's unity are evidently closely linked, and we are perhaps moving towards some understanding of what a many-layered matter unity could be in the early centuries. Some historians of an older generation – especially Anglicans – were fond of referring to 'the undivided Church of the first five centuries'; a phrase that will raise the eyebrows of the contemporary historian, familiar with the complex tensions and manifold variety of those centuries. But this is another case of the importance of having some familiar concepts 'made strange' for us by our historical studies. The early Church was deeply concerned about unity, yet the categories and arguments used to discuss it seem not to engage with the typically modern ways of staging the debates. Even something that may seem to us absolutely axiomatic, unanimity in the definition of the canon of Scripture, took some time to emerge. Churches quite rapidly came to recognise the irreducible importance of the unity of Jewish and Christian Scripture (they needed to argue from prophecy and to affirm the goodness of creation and of God's dealing with Israel); but a surprising number of loose ends survived as to the limits of Christian Scripture up to the fourth century (we know of unease in some quarters about Hebrews and Revelation, for example). Nor do we find an absolute homogeneity in patterns of church order or governance. We can say that by the early second century the churches of the Mediterranean world were generally led by bishops, presiding over a college of elders; but the way this worked in a city like Antioch and the way it worked in a city like Alexandria were very different − not to mention the sensitive question of how it worked in Rome, where there is evidence that it took longer for a single 'episcopal' figure to emerge.[26]

More surprisingly, we find traces of quite significant divergence over sacramental practice. The question of whether those who had left the fellowship of the mainstream Church and then returned, or had received baptism in a dissident group and later asked for admittance to the mainstream body, should be rebaptised caused considerable debate in the third century, and it is clear that not every church had the same view. For some, like the North African bishop Cyprian, baptism made no sense except as an initiation into the fellowship of the 'catholic' church, so that anyone coming from elsewhere needed baptism.[27] For others in the same period, like Dionysius of Alexandria, it was possible to recognise that a valid induction into the Body of Christ had taken place, even if the induction was concretely into a body that was in error or schism. But it is also Dionysius who argues that mutual denunciations or excommunications between churches on this matter would be wrong; local communities develop diverse customs, and the weight of local discernment and tradition should not be discounted.[28]

We should not overstate these divergences in reaction against the blandness of earlier pictures of patristic harmony, but they need to be recognised if only to stop us running away with the idea that the early Church's unity is something that can be reduced to the kind of formula that might satisfy most ecumenical negotiators of the modern age. What appears is a diverse assortment of what I have elsewhere called 'skills of recognition' and practices by which exchange between churches is sustained and built up. By the third century (probably earlier), the simple custom of circular letters announcing the election of a new bishop and asking for prayers had become a standard feature of much Mediterranean church life, as had the circulation of disciplinary decisions, drawing out the complementary genre of letters to new bishops promising fellowship and prayer, and sometimes letters endorsing or challenging disciplinary enactments. The accumulation of collections of letters like these formed an important element in the archives of local churches and the dossiers of individual bishops; an historian like Eusebius is able to utilise such dossiers to good effect, as he makes clear in his biographical treatment of Dionysius of Alexandria in particular.[29] To be excluded from this routine circulation of information and from the assurances of mutual prayers was – in the absence of any organ for universally enforceable discipline – the main form of sanction and protest between churches.

But we should remember also that the earliest rationale we have for the circulation of letters between local churches is to share news about persecution and martyrdom. From the letters of Ignatius of Antioch on his way to execution at the very beginning of the second century to the letter of the church in Smyrna describing Polycarp's death, from Dionysius' letters about the sufferings of the Alexandrian church to the letter of Phileas of Thmuis in Egypt during the great persecution of the first decade of the fourth century,[30] martyr narratives are a very substantial part of the common currency of the early Church. It is not too much to say that the appeal for mutual recognition of the experience of martyrdom is one of the primitive components of the Church's unity. The church that writes from Smyrna or Lyons to share the record of significant deaths at the hands of imperial power is inviting another church to acknowledge that they see in these things the signs of Christ's sacred royal power and of the alien citizenship that defines the Church's difference.

The unity of the earliest centuries, then, lies partly in this mutual recognition of language grounded in a common sense of holiness, suffering and sovereignty. The implicit test for a church as to whether it belongs in the framework of catholic fellowship is whether it knows how to resist, whether it speaks and behaves as an assembly answerable to the emperor's Lord rather than just the emperor. If the discussion in this chapter is along the right lines, later doctrinal refinement is an effort to fill out a little what it means to speak, not only to behave (and suffer), as foreign citizens, what establishes and vindicates the conviction of having another citizenship. So, as I have suggested, we make the best sense of doctrine in the historical context of the early Church if we see it as an exegesis of martyrdom; with martyrdom itself being an exegesis, a lived exposition, of taking Christ seriously as the one through whom the definition of God's people has been changed. Among God's new people, the way in which citizenship is most clearly manifested is in risking one's life on behalf of the sovereignty of Jesus; when the most obvious risks seem to be past, that sovereignty still needs unpacking and exploration; and its implications for a post-martyrdom period have to be followed through, whether in the analyses of contemplation by the monastic fathers or in the theology of unceasing self-scrutiny, confession and penitence found in Augustine.

IV

In conclusion, then, can we properly draw out anything from this examination for understanding the integrity of the Church now? The early Church cannot function for us in quite the way it did for some of our forebears, as a paradigm of untroubled unanimity, occasionally disrupted by deliberate and sinful perversions of revealed truth by individual heretics. Nor can we simply set the early Church before us as a model to be reproduced, stripping away any forms of worship, ministry or theological idiom not found before the fourth or fifth Christian century. For good or ill, we know a little more about how the history of the early Church was actually constructed and about the nature of the conflicts that arose, and are less likely to settle for a story in which doctrinal controversy only ever arises because of the rebellious malice of pride-filled individuals.

But to know all this should not involve us in a cynical assumption that the record of patristic doctrinal evolution is a mixture of arbitrary power struggle and abstract ideological refinement. The question of where holiness was to be found was an urgent and real issue in a society where holiness was almost universally believed to be located in political power: the pressure to define and refine, in ways the modern student cannot immediately identify with, is not a light matter in such a world. And in the last century or so, it is significant that believers have from time to time had to confront just such pressure when the alliance of political power and a kind of religious mythology recreates something of the atmosphere of the Roman empire. Thus when in 1936 the Confessing Church in Germany, the network of those who resisted the anti-Semitic legislation of the Third Reich, bound itself to the 'Barmen Declaration', affirming the sovereignty of God in Christ over all other claims to authority, the primitive shape of Christian self-definition became visible once more.[31] Likewise in South Africa in the 1980s, the 'Kairos Document' (modelled in some measure on Barmen) declared the Church's judgement against apartheid and defined the theological case for apartheid as heresy, the impulse was that of Polycarp in the arena.[32] A higher court than the human was being invoked, and invoked against human courts that surrounded their dealings with a religious aura, either pagan, as in the Third Reich, or pseudo-biblical, as in the South African Nationalist Party.

In other words, it is still true that the Church will at times find its unity when it finds what it has to resist. The stories of Barmen and the South African church are, so to speak, worked examples of where resistance has come to be imperative. But much more broadly, we continue to tell stories of the martyrs to refresh our sense of what the Church distinctively is; and the twentieth century has, notoriously, produced more martyrs than any other. One of the most remarkable facts of recent Christian history is the willingness for an ecumenism in thinking about martyrdom. More and more we celebrate each other's witnesses and do not ask too closely about their denominational allegiance. The statues of the martyrs on the west front of Westminster Abbey and the Chapel of the Martyrs of the Twentieth Century in Canterbury Cathedral include Orthodox, Protestant and Catholic figures side by side; and there is a growing number of books for liturgical reference that do the same.

This may suggest that we are moving decisively away from one sort of misleading form of reflection about martyrs. It is possible to tell stories of martyrdom to prove we are right and others are wrong; the more martyrs, the more secure we shall feel (and the terrible end of that logic is the mindset of the suicide bomber). Or we can tell such stories to induce different sorts of guilt, to intensify the emotional charge of a Christianity that might otherwise look rather dull. But these are not theological ways of considering martyrdom; they are – in the most pejorative sense – political. A theological discourse about this subject would be one in which we simply say, 'Here is the novel manifestation of holy power which is the ground of our being here at all as a distinctive and recognisable community.' This is why we speak of another citizenship and another sovereignty.

And in the context of modern resistance – as in the Barmen Declaration – we can still see how the need to find words for the distance and integrity of the Christian community produces renewed affirmations about creation and about Jesus Christ. The early Church does not give us a pattern of perfect life and language, but it does emphatically show us the connection between the risk and cost of an alien citizenship and the necessary words to speak about Christ.

So, if it is not clear why we should be bothered about our fidelity to the formulations of Nicaea or Chalcedon, this analysis of the first Christian centuries may revive our sense that, whatever the conceptual toughness or oddity of the language used in these creeds and definitions, this was the least that could properly be said about the basis of the *ekklesia* as such, the sort of thing which, if *not* said, would alter drastically the Church's claim to be free to appeal beyond the powers of this world and to deny the ascription of unqualified holiness to any system of earthly government. To develop a point made elsewhere, if the language of the creeds is difficult for us, this may be less a function of its intrinsic conceptual problems and more a comment on the weakened urgency felt about our Christian identity and mission.

But there is a further point to reflect on as well. The early Church took some time to formulate its doctrinal positions, and it was increasingly careful to warn against a reading of doctrinal statements that saw them as providing some kind of definition of what is involved in being God, definitions of divine 'essence'. What emerged was a minimum recipe for sane and resourceful Christian speech. Attempts to establish other elements as needing to be included in such minimal stipulations will have to consider whether these are matters that likewise can be seen as essential to a rationale for martyrdom and its claims. This is the sort of question that, I suggest, has to be asked in the context of the theological 'culture wars' that currently affect most of the churches, not least the Anglican Communion. An innovation is proposed; and the question about it should not be, 'Is this a step towards an uncontroversial modernising of faith and practice, a step towards "inclusion" or "pluralism"?' but, 'Is this something without which we could not, in the long run, make sense of the commitments that make sense of martyrdom?' Or: an innovation is resisted; and the question should not be, 'Is this alien to our habits of interpretation?' but, 'Is this going to make it impossible to make sense of the Christian claim to an independent citizenship?' Some become nervous when debates about, say, the ordination of women or of gay people turn into claims and counter-claims about new practices implying a 'new religion'; but there is a necessary element of such a contest in any serious discussion about fresh developments in Christian identity, and the issues are not trivial. They need discussion in terms of theology, not politics or PR; though they also need scrutiny to protect us from the melodramatic error of treating every aspect of Christian discourse as equally definitive. There are (as is abundantly clear) no short answers; but an informed awareness of our Christian origins at least offers some tools for reflection and some instances of mistaken identification of where fundamentals lie. I shall want to explore this further in the final chapter of this book.

Perhaps the most uncomfortable suggestion that might arise from these thoughts is that we may not know the answers to some of our contemporary and agonising dilemmas without the quite specific and concrete challenge that could come from an authority claiming ultimate and sacred authority. I have mentioned the German Confessing Church: one of the notable features of that network was that it brought together Protestants of both Lutheran and Reformed tradition, people who had been separated for several centuries and had not shared sacramental fellowship. Powerful disagreements over the eucharist and Christology and the doctrine of grace had divided them very seriously. Yet in the face of the Third Reich, it was clear to those who formed the Confessing network that which side you might take on these issues did not after all determine whether or not you could make sense of the Church's identity as Church, as a body obedient to the invitation of Jesus and looking to his authority first of all. The existence of the Confessing Church did not resolve the bitter historic disputes; nor, sadly, did the alliance of the two Protestant families simply take off from this point. The network had a chequered history and what happened in the German churches after the war was not dictated by this experience in the way one might have hoped and prayed. Yet a moment of extraordinary grace and vision was given in crisis; and that cannot be forgotten.

What is sobering is the thought that we might not discover exactly what orthodoxy involves, short of a major crisis or threat. But what is of abiding importance is to hold on to the sense that this is where and why the Church's self-definition *matters*. To be clear about the Church's boundaries can become an obsessive concern with knowing exactly who is outside, who can be trusted to reflect orthodoxy as I have learned it. But definition matters, ultimately, so that resistance is possible to the idolatrous claims of total power that may be made from time to time in the world. Definition matters so that the Christian is free to say with conviction that the truth of the world and of humanity is not at the disposal of this or that system of political management. And precisely because it is crisis that brings certain things to light, we are reminded that the Church's integrity, orthodoxy or whatever is a gift, not primarily an achievement. Inevitably, the Church becomes involved in patrolling its boundaries; not every spirit is of Christ, not every way of speaking and acting is capable of being transparent to Christ. Discipline is exercised, so that what is said and done in the Church displays its accountability. But when all justice has been done to this need, an area of reserve remains: we do not yet know what will be drawn out of us by the pressure of Christ's reality, what the full shape of a future orthodoxy might be.

This is different from the rather glib way in which we sometimes speak of how new truths will be brought to light by the onward march of human understanding. Of such language, the Christian has the right to be somewhat suspicious; it has elements of truth, but moves us away from the early Christian conviction that it is in conflict with the pressures of the world that we learn most clearly what are the pressures of Christ. What is hard is discerning accurately where the pressures of the world are to be identified; and this is not at all the simple confrontation of 'left' and 'right' in theology or ethics that it is sometimes made out to be. The pressures of the world may be rightly seen in, let us say, an uncritical fascination with management and success; but also in a sentimental refusal to work accountably. They may be seen in an indifferent attitude to abortion; but also in high-octane campaigns for public moral purity. In a general environment of emotional and individualistic thinking about ethics, it is hardly surprising if Christians are often at sea when it comes to articulating what they think are the distinctive virtues the Church should be nourishing.

Be that as it may, this chapter has suggested that understanding the doctrinal and disciplinary struggles of the earliest Christian centuries pushes at us quite hard the imperative of grasping the Church's identity in terms of the difference that is made by the priority of what God does, the action of God in establishing his authority through the events of Christ's life, death and resurrection; martyrdom marks that difference. And in the light of this, it may be possible to look afresh at a later epoch in our history, to see if these primitive anxieties are in any way to be traced there – and, if they are, what new light this casts on the framing of their doctrinal and disciplinary turmoils. So we shall turn next to the Reformation era.

GRACE ALONE:
CONTINUITY AND NOVELTY
IN THE REFORMATION ERA

I

The first Christian centuries attempted to define a basic vocabulary for being Christian – or rather, for being a church, a distinctive social body given coherence by the action of God in Jesus. It did so partly in response to the reality of confrontation with the social order in which it was located – in response to martyrdom; it was trying to make sense of new forms of belonging together which were seen as subversive by the Roman Empire.

But in the centuries that followed the fourth-century legalisation of Christian practice and its imposition as the norm of behaviour for citizens of the empire, the Church had increasingly come to define itself as the natural and legitimate form of social life; it was simply not possible to define it in the terms that had made sense in the pre-Constantinian period.[1] In the East, where the empire survived after a fashion in the Byzantine world, the Church was an organic part of the close-woven fabric of public life held together by the sacred person of the *basileus*, the emperor 'reigning with Christ', to use a formulation that appears in official enactments.[2] In the West, after the collapse of imperial administration and the advent of the new Germanic kingdoms, the Church itself became a virtual successor state to the Roman Empire, the one political body in sight which provided a model of rational and law-governed life that was not limited to custom and local royal power but appealed to a universal standard of right. Organised with increasing sophistication in a network or pyramid of courts, with a supreme magistracy in Rome, the Church both supported and relativised the kingdoms in which it worked, providing a literate civil service, a body of 'clerks', but also insisting that the liberties of the clerical body were carefully negotiated in relation to the international system whose focus was the court of Rome. This could and did provoke bitter conflict – Henry II and Becket – but it was undeniably a coherent political pattern. It is worth remembering that the medieval Western Church, so far from being an apologist for mindless absolutism, was the chief guardian of the very idea of rights that were more than local and contractual. St Thomas Aquinas has been described, not entirely facetiously, as the first Whig, in the sense that he holds to a clear (classically rooted) doctrine of the responsibility of the executive power to principles guaranteed by someone other than the executive.[3]

Of course, this depended on a view of the Church in which its identity was specified in relation to its own professional class – 'religious persons' as opposed to 'secular', those who accepted the obligations of being (so to speak) citizens of the international 'state' of the ordained and the monastically professed as opposed to the baptised in general. In a situation where clerics were manifestly the guardians of legal order, this was not surprising; but it was a theologically uncomfortable aspect of medieval Western church life. The concept of the Body of Christ as the communion of baptised believers sat uneasily alongside the powerful assumption in politics and canon law that the Church was first the body of 'religious persons', the corporation of clerks. And the more that the Church was bound to this sort of identity, the more it was threatened by developments in European society which began to offer an alternative account and model of legal stability. What if the corporation of clerks was not the only body that could guarantee good government and clear legal principle? What if the authority of the 'secular' ruler was in fact God-given, not just the rather wobbly summit of a pyramid of feudal obligations? The emergence of a strong doctrine of princely authority, in Italy's city states and also north of the Alps in the Holy Roman Empire, combined with the emergence of a literate non-ordained class of lawyers and administrators, posed a serious challenge to the Church's monopoly of political legitimacy.

By the beginning of the sixteenth century, there was ample material for a crisis to develop. The legal and political issues just sketched were not thought about in a vacuum, and the loss of moral and legal credibility on the part of the late medieval and Renaissance papacy made the questions more urgent. If the papacy behaved as merely the tool of certain parties in European conflicts or as just another self-interested local princedom in Italy, it was not surprising that its rights as a disinterested international magistracy did not look very plausible. And this meant in turn that its authority as an arbiter of theological disputes was bound to come into question. The Reformation, when it happened, was neither simply about theological disagreement, nor simply about the papacy over against emerging princely states; it was both (and more), because of a lack of confidence in the papacy as an institution that could plausibly solve problems.

In what follows, it is important to keep in mind this interweaving of political and theological crises. To the extent that the Reformation is the revival of a long-dormant anxiety about the Church's identity, both the political and the theological elements of this anxiety are essential for an understanding of what was going on, just as in the patristic period. Thus, in regard to the political and social, what happened in the sixteenth century was, as a modern American scholar, Debra Shuger, has argued persuasively, the pushing of the Church towards the 'interstices' of public life, because it could no longer claim to *be* itself the space in which public life was conducted.[4] This is the sense in which it is true to say that the Reformation was the dawn of 'secularisation' (that weasel word); but it was, just as significantly, the moment when it became possible to ask again about the distinctiveness of the Church. As Shuger suggests, it is as the

Church moves towards the interstices that it begins again to see its task as to imagine an alternative culture or community. It is no longer disputing the ground of practical control of the public sphere, and so it concentrates upon what makes it *not* the same as the prevailing environment. And this holds true for both Catholic and Protestant communities in the wake of the sixteenth-century crisis.

This prompts a caution too about the ready use of those two familiar words, Catholic and Protestant – though I have not found easy alternatives in these pages. Following the principle already stressed that a good historical perspective makes the familiar strange, we need to bear in mind that the Reformation debate was not one between self-designated Catholics and Protestants; it was a debate about where the Catholic Church was to be found. 'Is the Pope a Catholic?' was not a joke in the sixteenth century. The objection to the medieval Church articulated by the Reformers was that it had ceased to *be* a church in any theologically interesting sense; and as we shall see, this has a great deal to do with an instinctive recovery by the Reformers – and subsequently by their critics too – of the patristic conviction about the dependence of the Church on God's action alone. What had prevented the Church being itself for all these centuries was, in the eyes of the Reformers, a forgetfulness about the truth that the Church did not exist either by human decision or by a kind of divine delegation of powers to the visible ecclesial body, but by the direct will and agency of God. Any community failing to believe and embody this failed the test of being 'Catholic' and had to be regarded as a community of human and legal solidarity alone: hence the many unfriendly variants of 'popish' to describe the unreformed church.

But this is to run ahead somewhat. I want to return for a moment to the point just prior to the open protests of Luther, to look at some further factors in the political and cultural situation which may throw light on those protests. This is harder to document accurately and fully; but cultural historians have sometimes noted the parallel development in the fifteenth and early sixteenth centuries of – on the one hand – immense elaboration in the world of public symbolic ceremony, of social and ritual conduct, and artistic convention (visual and musical), and – on the other – the emphasis in some spiritual movements of the day upon sobriety and simplicity, individual faithfulness to inner discipline and so on.[5] It is the juxtaposition of the ceremonial of the Burgundian court or the Field of the Cloth of Gold, the music of Ockeghem or Fayrfax with the *Imitation of Christ* or the piety of Dean Colet and the young Erasmus. The public world becomes more and more heavily structured, overdetermined, and the inner space of the moral and spiritual agent more and more austerely isolated and guarded. It would be wrong to speak of a sceptical dimension coming in, but there is a degree of inner disengagement from some aspects of public theatre on the part of the self-consciously morally serious. The closely scrutinised private conscience – informed of course by doctrine and biblical meditation – is the focus of concern. And this is not simply a question of withdrawal from actual public activity: those who belong in this world make their forays into the world of public business and seek to influence the powerful (Dean Colet at one point made a not too successful attempt to challenge Henry VIII's foreign policy).[6] It is sometimes forgotten that the 'public' for Reformation argument included large numbers of people who had an extensive 'humanist' education which disposed them, both in style and moral emphasis, to be discontented with the aesthetics of the late medieval Church and the late medieval public square.

To revert to the terms sketched in our first chapter, one of the things that was happening was that the forms of the Church's visible life had ceased to be obvious, manifestly natural. That is to say, they were ripe for something like historical critique. As the factors outlined above converged, it became more obviously possible to see the Church's life as extended in time and vulnerable to the passage of time: to see it as involving loss and error, in a way not so clearly possible during the preceding millennium. What was the Church if it turned out not to be the guarantor of public, legal and symbolic order? And what was the theological status of that order itself if it was not simply determined by 'clerks'? The supposed problem of 'church–state relations' in this period needs to be handled with great care, as it is more correctly a problem about the nature and definition of authority in the Church itself than about the relations between two neatly separate, already defined entities. And even where the theological debates of the era do not seem to be directly about the character of the Church as a modern theologian might think of it, this is often the hidden impetus. Behind the details of controversy the same concern is regularly to be heard: in what sense is this a 'supernatural' society, one whose justification is provided by God alone?

II

Luther's theology is shaped by all the things we have been considering. It is moved along by the process of reading the Bible with some of the 'humanist' tools of the day; it is deeply bound up with issues around political legitimacy and authority; it is not – contrary to the historical myth still prevalent in liberal Europe – a bid for individual freedom of conscience, but it *is* a protest against the belief that conscientious scruple can be solved by immediate human authority; and it is triggered by a theological abuse directly attributable to papal ambition (though Luther himself does not immediately make the connection).

What it places at the centre of everything is the gratuity, almost the arbitrariness, of God's action. Luther himself, describing the evolution of his theology, identifies the major breakthrough with a moment of new understanding concerning the Bible's language about God's 'justice'. He had previously thought of this as that in virtue of which God has the right to condemn sinners, and had accordingly feared and hated this language; but he suddenly came to see – with real help from the new style of biblical interpretation beginning to develop in response to the new availability of the Bible in its original languages – that it should be read as expressing what God does for us. Just as, when we hear of the wisdom of God in the Bible, for example, we think of how God's action makes us wise, so when we hear of God's justice we should think of that act by which he makes us just. God's justice is, in other words, not God's 'reaction' to our behaviour or the implacable standard by which he judges us, but his initiative, quite irrespective of our behaviour. God is free to do what he wills, and his freedom takes the form of acting so as to change us. It is a serious mistake to think that Luther (or any other classical Protestant) believed that 'justification' meant only a change in God's attitude without effect in us. On the contrary, what changes is that we become the locus of God's free activity. Unprovoked, unconditioned and unconstrained by any other agent, God steps into the void and chaos of created existence and establishes himself there as God.[7]

Hence Luther's passion about the centrality of the cross. Where could we more perfectly see this 'strange work' of God but in the place where the wretchedness of the created world and the total failure of human resource or human virtue is most fully exhibited? Where else could we see God's absolute liberty to be God, irrespective of any external conditions? And where but in our own empty and hellish dereliction could we find what it is to trust without reserve in God's freedom exercised for our sake?[8] What gives us ground to stand before God is God: God has in Christ taken his stand in the human world and answered for, taken responsibility for, every human being, quite apart from any achievement or aspiration on the part of humans.

And accordingly, the definition of the Church becomes rather different from what had been taken for granted (one of Luther's earliest and most intelligent Catholic critics, Cardinal Cajetan, had observed that Luther's theology implied a 'new church' because it refused to accept the conventional problem-solving mechanisms of appeal to customary and canonical authority).[9] No element of the Church's structure could give assurance of God's promise and act, for that would be to imply that God's freedom had somehow been mortgaged to the actions and decisions of the Church. The Church remains a sacramental community (another recurrent mistake in reading Luther is to misrepresent his theology of the sacraments as a denial of the very idea of sacraments) – that is, it is a place where a community is gathered around specific actions in which the promise of God is declared to be present and effective (actions which now include the proclamation of God's action in preaching as well as the witness of baptism and eucharist). But the effectiveness is not in the form of word or action; it is in the presence of the foundational word of Christ which the community witnesses to. The Catholic Church is simply that gathering in which what Christ has promised is spoken and heard.

It should be clear (and it was fairly promptly made clear in the sixteenth century) that this decisively undermined any residual notion that the Church was essentially a kind of state, a legal order or guarantor of legal order. This was, it might be said, a theological vision well equipped to make sense of a church in the 'interstices'. But to state matters in these terms is actually not helpful. It can lead to yet another caricature of Lutheran thought. It is not that the Church retreats to the margins, concentrated simply upon what happens when the community gathers for worship and proclamation, while 'outside' it the world goes on its way. If the Christian believer has become the place where divine action happens, we may expect that divine action overflows in active service to the entire world, a service which cannot be anything but Christlike in form. Freed from the obsessive need to make myself acceptable to God, I may now be, without anxiety, at the disposal of all. The rather odd notion that Lutheran theology means that ethical issues are not of fundamental concern in the Church or that human political virtue has nothing to do with the gospel is a distortion, though it is one that the later Luther sometimes invites by his insistent refusal to consider virtue a foundation for divine action and to allow the clergy to exercise political power.[10]

The Church here is most fundamentally the community of the baptised; and to be baptised is to be identified as a witness to

God's gratuitous action. For Luther, this implied that certain theologies more or less invalidated any claim to be a church. Obviously the pseudo-political model of the Western Middle Ages, with its focus on a clerical elite governed by a supreme ecclesiastical magistrate made no sense; but neither did a community that laid down stringent conditions of behaviour separating it from the public life around, nor a community that refused infant baptism on the grounds that conscious faith was required (that is to make conditions for God) nor a community which promised or insisted upon specific subjective experiences of God. Luther was as hostile to the radical Reformers as he was to the papal church, for exactly the same reason, that he believed they set limits to God's liberty. Instead of the Church being a community in which God's action was the ground and focus of everything, the Church became, in these groups, a community that was set apart primarily by human, visible differentiating factors – distinctive behaviour, special feelings. And this was simply to reintroduce an idolatrous view of the Church as a community able to appeal for its difference and its legitimation to something other than God, to establish the Church as a human elite.

The typical worries of the Reformed churches arose from this powerful and problematic first principle. For Luther, if the Church was not the fiefdom of a clerical elite, its government depended in some degree on the 'secular' magistrate – not as a figure external to the Church, but as a member of the Church to whom a specific vocation had been given. Lutherans developed a strong doctrine of the lay ruler's vocation as a governor of the external affairs of the church; in the English Reformation this was even more marked, with a good deal of deployment of Old Testament texts about the Kings of Israel.[11] But this assumed that the ruler was a reliable member of a church that had experienced reform; what if this were not the case? The followers of Calvin were readier to argue a strong case for the body of believers exercising in some way the kingly rule of Christ, and thus having the liberty to call rulers to account.

How could the Church witness to God's freedom if it were in any way under the control of an unconverted ruler? God's absolute freedom to predestine his creatures to life or death was, for the Calvinist system, an axiomatic consequence of belief in God's freedom to act for our salvation. What authority could therefore be granted to a ruler or ruling class who did not belong among the elect? Calvinists came up with varying solutions to the practical conundrums involved here, some defending the right of the elect to use force in a struggle against unreformed political authority, some looking to the imposition by law of biblical codes of behaviour.[12] But the underlying problem is to do with the basic Reformation principle: the Church must be judged by its freedom to witness to the freedom of God. That this could produce dramatically diverse attitudes to existing government should not blind us to the way in which a theological revolution, partly grounded in the wider political crisis sketched earlier in this chapter, had reopened the whole issue of how and why the Church was *different*.

The impact of this upon the continuing papal church would need longer consideration than can be given here. But it would be true to say that the same issue of difference is no less at stake. Once the 'naturalness' of the medieval religio-political settlement had evaporated, once the Church was no longer in the same sense the guarantor of the legitimacy of governance, the Church had no option but to look to its own credibility and thus to its loyalty to certain standards and requirements. Counter-Reformation Catholicism intensified the control of the hierarchy over parish clergy and female religious orders, standardised training for the priesthood and made some effort to regain or reassert the pope's role as arbiter of legal sovereignty (Pius V's excommunication of Elizabeth I and release of her subjects from allegiance is the most dramatic case in point).

But the paradoxical effect of the new Catholic order after the Council of Trent was to underline the distance between the clerical corporation – centralised, disciplined and professionalised as never before – and the power elites of the new

European states. By the middle of the seventeenth century, while papal Catholicism had made an extraordinary recovery in terms of numerical allegiance across Europe (especially central and eastern Europe), it had been obliged to accept a new status in the political world, as one of several formally legitimate religious bodies. It continued to argue in theory against religious pluralism, but in practice had no option but to collaborate with a very different religious environment. Its efforts in the sixteenth century to clarify its distinctive identity succeeded in preserving a clear set of markers over against Protestantism and over against 'secular' power; but it, no less than the Protestant communities, had become accustomed to living in the interstices.[13] The dissonance between this reality and some of the theological language that continued to be current steadily pushed the Roman Catholic Church towards the immense corporate self-examination of the Second Vatican Council, where there was at last a theological recognition of the proper and inevitable plurality of religious commitments that could freely exist within a single political society.[14] The Roman Catholic Church had acknowledged that it, no less than the Protestant communities, had come to rest in the interstices of a society that believed itself to have found other ways of dealing with legitimacy.

These are themes we shall be revisiting later. My present point is that the whole of the Western Christian world was affected by the sixteenth-century revival of issues about what made the Church distinctively the Church – by the 'making strange' of Christian identity that emerged in and from the complex crisis of early modernity. Studying the history of the Reformation, like studying the early Church, does not give us simple and authoritative models for our vision of the Church now, but it does offer a hint as to the kinds of circumstance that provoke most deeply this question of identity and some of the theological resources that could be deployed in response. As we have seen, the belief that the Church was a community whose sole ultimate rationale was the gratuitous act of God became the governing principle of various reconstructed local churches.

But we should not too quickly assume that the response to this challenge on the part of the continuing Catholic community, or those at any rate who resisted a wholesale allegiance to radical reform, was necessarily at odds with such an emphasis. Luther already acknowledges the ambiguities of doctrines of the Church that take their stand on ground other than the bald fact of baptism. And the revived Catholicism of the Council of Trent and the new religious orders represented a tacit acceptance of the need to make visible the priority of grace as something more disturbing than a simple sacralising of existing order.

The disruptive elements in Christian piety were not less in evidence in Catholic than in Lutheran and Reformed practice in this era. The researches of Michel de Certeau have drawn out the way in which the Catholic imagination of the period began to reshape the very self-awareness of the believer – and indeed to shape the characteristic self-image of modernity. Many of the major texts of Catholic spirituality in the Counter-Reformation era, the texts we call 'mystical', above all the writings of the Spanish Carmelites, Teresa of Avila and John of the Cross, depict a human self that is radically unstable and incomplete, struggling to find a way of representing itself. It is inescapably, essentially, a self that is homeless in the world, trained to be suspicious of any sense of gratification and completion, trained to scrutinise both feeling and thought, to be for itself a problem, an object to be examined sceptically. In the writings of the mystics, this is of course part of a process in which the self learns that its security is in God and that 'religious experience' as much as worldly success or stability is irrelevant to this deepest anchorage. It has a good deal in common with Luther's determination to tear the self away from a quest for its own centre and ground it in a wholly alien yet wholly accepting divine initiative. But, as Certeau says, if that alien love is removed from the picture, what is left is the characteristically modern self, desiring, dissatisfied, homeless.[15]

It is a further turn of the screw in the process we have already been looking at. The heart of Christian identity seems here to be an intense scepticism, an acknowledgement of the fact that at the centre of every human reality is an absence. It is a vision already powerfully at work in Augustine, centuries earlier, but only coming to fruition in the social turmoil of the early modern age. When the idea of a sacred order guaranteed by the visible institutions of the Church disappears, something happens not only to society but also to the individual. The developments that flow from this period involve both the erosion of arbitrary authority in society and the restlessly anxious attempt to find some firm ground for the self and its knowledge and liberty – Descartes' awareness of the thinking self, the Enlightenment appeal to universal reason, Kant's mapping of what we cannot but take for granted in our thinking and evaluating, and so on. Late modernity in turn dissolves these solutions, leaving the essential groundlessness of the self and its certainty or liberty or continuity exposed.

It is almost as though the Lutheran and Carmelite argument, like that of Augustine himself, is a sort of pre-emptive strike in this history. Suppose the worst, suppose a void at the heart of humanity, a lack of any principle of continuity or integrity in the self; yes, but this is precisely where the alien claim of God's gift makes itself clear. The identity of the Christian, the identity of the Church, emerges – as never before – as an issue that has to do with the identity of humanity itself.

To say that this is a high-risk step in the intellectual life of the Western Christian world is an understatement. The shadows are there from the start. Luther's confused and inconclusive wrestling with the translation of the Gospel's imperatives into public and social life is a well-intentioned effort to make clear a valid and important point. The Church is not society's policeman; the law of a state is not by definition the pattern of Christlikeness which constitutes the community of believers. But the implication of this *can* be that the world sorts out its conflicts by an admittedly often tragic pragmatism, by seeking lesser evils only. The individual believer is indeed for Luther a true and free agent of Christ's service to the world, but God ordains coercion for society at large (which is not composed exclusively of true believers). It is a point that resurfaces very interestingly in seventeenth-century England: Anglican apologists like Lancelot Andrewes criticise Roman Catholic thinking for licensing the clergy to exercise political power (and, a very immediate consideration in his context, to subvert existing systems of power), and they argue the superior virtue of the English Reformed Church on the grounds that it does not soil its hands with violence. Yet this stands alongside an active and untroubled defence of state violence (torture and execution) against dissidents. Something has come adrift in this argumentation.[16]

The Church in the interstices can, it seems, become a Church that passively sanctions anything the existing system of power may do, especially if that existing system endorses the Church's right to pursue its 'spiritual' life. And in something of the same way, the cutting loose of the believing self from any interior anchorage could and did produce cultures of complacency and static formalism. Luther and others revolted against a world in which 'religious' duties could so multiply as to squeeze out the basic imperatives of compassion and social support; medieval piety, as they saw it, blurred the boundaries between these fundamental human duties (including family loyalties) and the huge quantity of merit-earning ritual actions that could secure divine favour. But for a superficial hearer, this might be simply an affirmation of the most immediate and undemanding loyalties. Historic Protestantism, in Britain, Germany and elsewhere, has an embarrassing record of collusion with uncritical nationalism, stifling social conformism and patriarchy, narrow class-dominated attitudes. Too many German Lutherans stood by uneasily as their country descended into barbarism in the 1930s, and some stood by no less ineffectually as the rhetoric of cold war developed in the fifties, and criticised those (like Karl Barth) who mounted theological arguments against the nuclear arms race.[17] Anglicans defended the providential status of the British Empire and echoed the worst of anti-German rabble-rousing in the First World War.[18] This sort of religion has sanctioned people's social and political comfort zones: a very paradoxical effect to come from Luther's radical terror and trust in the face of God. It is a paradox wonderfully caught in Auden's sonnet, 'Luther'.

> With conscience cocked to listen for the thunder,
> He saw the Devil busy in the wind,
> Over the chiming steeples and then under
> The doors of nuns and doctors who had sinned.
>
> What apparatus could stave off disaster
> Or cut the brambles of man's error down?
> Flesh was a silent dog that bites its master,
> World a still pond in which its children drown.
>
> The fuse of Judgement spluttered in his head:
> 'Lord, smoke these honeyed insects from their hives.
> All Works, Great Men, Societies are bad.
> The Just shall live by Faith . . .' he cried in dread.
>
> And men and women of the world were glad,
> Who'd never cared or trembled in their lives.[19]

The Reformers wanted above all to do away with the idea that the Church was a human community in competition with others; its integrity lay not in its capacity to hold its own in the world's territory but in its faithfulness to the creative act of God. The cost of this was to undermine both the Church's freedom to challenge other human communities and the significance of those patient long-term practices of rite and prayer that might keep alive the sense of indebtedness to God. The result was often a politically subservient Church and a bourgeois, undemanding piety. Yet the Catholic response could seem like a reinforcement of the idea that the difference of the Church was a matter of tribal habits and a clear line of clerical authority, confronting the modern state with a sort of resentment and fighting for a maximum amount of space within its structures.

Neither side succeeds in capturing the distinctiveness bound up with the different 'sovereignty' discussed in the preceding chapter. And we should not expect it to be otherwise. The history of the Reformation and its aftermath illustrates the degree to which it is impossible to write the Church's history as a story about the Church's reflection on itself in the abstract. When the complex narrative of society overall puts in front of the Church a question that has not been asked in *those* terms before, the Church has considerable resources to deploy – but in the nature of the case has very little sense of what the long-term cost of this or that strategy of response might be. As in any ecological system, we are not likely to know the degree and character of the effects of change immediately; there are inescapably tragic elements in this story, in the sense that unintended cost is never absent. And this might have something to say to current crises, even if only to commend a measure of that complement to the tragic vision which we call irony, the recognition that what is said and done by human beings routinely misses or misrepresents the whole range of meanings encoded in a situation.

III

Within this broad picture, there are one or two aspects of the English Reformation in particular that are worth looking at briefly, both as illustrating some of the more general points made and as indicating some of the resources already being used to counter misunderstanding. William Tyndale, right at the beginning of the English Reformation, has a very distinctive sense of how justification by faith shapes a moral and political agenda;[20] Richard Hooker, at the end of the sixteenth century, struggles to identify and refute a particular theology of the Church which, claiming to be the logical corollary of Reformed principle, in fact undermines it.[21]

Tyndale follows Luther quite closely in seeing the Christian's style of life as essentially the outworking of the 'alien' life within, the reality of Christ; he repeats Luther's point that the incarnate Lord was not merciful, generous, forgiving and so on in order to win approval from heaven, since heaven was his very environment. His good works are the expression of who he is. But Tyndale moves a little beyond Luther in seeking to clarify how this defines *specific* imperatives. There is nothing good in us that is not given; therefore we are, beyond all possibility of repayment, fundamentally *indebted*. But that awareness of indebtedness has the effect of making relative and questionable all our claims as human beings to have the right of disposal over what is concretely and materially ours.[22] This is not only a doctrine about spiritual goods.

What we believe we own is in fact given to us so that it may be shared: it is owed already to those whose need is greater – not only (as Tyndale controversially claimed) to our neighbours and fellow-citizens, but to those who are distant, even those who do not share our faith. Here at the beginning of the English Reformation, in fact, is one of the principles that should have established the impossibility of a bourgeois and nationalist interpretation of Christian identity. Although Tyndale follows Luther in deploring monastic piety (as diverting energies into a 'specialist' religious practice instead of transforming public life), and although he spells out at some length the duties of each person's station in society in ways that help to define classical Protestant ideas of social and family order, he also has this element of unsettling and radical universalism. It poses the question of what society would look like if the dominant motif in Christian life were gratitude, a detachment from possessions grounded not so much in any doctrine of the evils of this world's goods as in a recognition that God's gifts are restless in the hands of the receiver until they are given again, and that our rights of possession in and over the material world are systematically undermined by the awareness of the givenness of all things, spiritual and material.

Tyndale is not a systematic theologian but a preacher and moralist; yet we can begin to see what a systematic social ethic grounded in his Reformed priorities might involve. The theological principle of God's prior action in all things bound up in our relation to him here spills over into some extremely

Why Study the Past?

practical considerations. What is it to recognise in the concrete circumstances of one's own prosperity or welfare the presence of divine action? It is, Tyndale suggests, to recognise that the apparently static things that secure our prosperity are carriers of God's love, and that therefore they cannot sit still with us, they must not be prevented from being active signs of love. When we try to hold on to them, we make empty our claims to be dependent on God for our spiritual security, because we implicitly deny that God is active in *all* his gifts.

The extension of Christian obligation beyond immediate horizons relates, though not entirely straightforwardly, to the second of the English Reformed writers I want to consider. Hooker first attracted unfriendly attention for his defence of the idea that non-Reformed Christians might still in some sense belong in the Catholic Church (that Roman Catholics might still be Catholics).[23] He argues in sermons of the 1580s that it is risky to identify saving faith with conformity to a particular 'complete set' of confessional commitments: ingrained error, inherited assumptions and so on shape our conscious thoughts and beliefs about God and the Church, but it is misleading to see this as wholly invalidating a profession of faith. Why should not radical trust in the all-sufficiency of Christ's work coexist with mistaken, even gravely mistaken, ideas about the specific content of Christian doctrine?[24] Here and in later writings, he attempts to distinguish between faith as saving trust (which can coexist with various emotional and intellectual states and yet in its way be perfect) and faith as the concrete habit of mind in a human being, which is capable of growing or shrinking, of being more or less robust and more or less consciously embraced. It is a region of his thought where he sails closest to the wind from the point of view of strict Lutherans and Calvinists alike. But his rationale is entirely in accord with the priorities of the Reformation.

He is establishing two points, both of some interest for the present discussion. First, he is, in this as in other aspects of his work, granting some space for a positive theological attitude to the contingencies of history. Earlier generations of Christians have not, because of circumstance and habit and unchallenged custom, been able to confess what a sixteenth-century Protestant would regard as true doctrine. To say that this negates any possibility of their being truly members of Christ's Body would be, in Hooker's eyes, to place the theological emphasis in precisely the wrong place – as if the conscious human appropriation of true doctrine were the same as saving faith. If it were, the stress would be back on human agency rather than divine. To allow a degree of agnosticism about the Christian integrity of believers in past ages is to make an all-important disjunction between divine freedom to enter into relation with repentant and trusting human beings and the ways in which those human beings express or understand their own trust. Of course it *matters* here and now to know the difference between error and truth, orthodoxy and heresy; but that does not settle the issue of belonging in Christ.

So, second, the insistence by Hooker's Puritan critics that nothing short of a comprehensive restructuring of the Church according to strict biblical principle counts as true reformation is likewise to be seen as a shifting of emphasis from God to the human. The Bible does not in fact (Hooker believed) legislate clearly and unconditionally in matters of church order; the Church has had to discern and develop, and accepting such historical discernment is not infidelity to Scripture. Much in the Reformed Church of England is a matter of contingent provision arising from what has been deemed proper and made lawful. To argue against this is to risk, once again, confusing the issue as to where the definition of the Church is to be found. Hooker has this at least in common with Luther, that he is profoundly suspicious of conditions other than baptism as a test of belonging in the Church; and he is in effect saying to his opponents that they are not Protestant enough, if the touchstone of Protestantism is witness to the liberty and priority of God's act.[25]

If both Tyndale and Hooker are unhappy with certain ways of putting limits on Christian obligation and Christian recognition, it is not because they hold to some modern ideal of comprehensiveness or inclusivity. They are rigorous and sometimes rigorist in their understanding of the Church's claims, and they are professional polemicists who believe with all their hearts that error and false doctrine must be combated. But they are clear about the danger of a Protestantism that has lost sight of its own original radicalism, its own commitment to the alien and unexpected initiative of God. Of course, Hooker too is embedded in a history that is full of ambiguities; of course his work is closely associated with a highly political campaign designed to intensify the persecution of Puritan dissidents by Elizabeth's government.[26] But of all the arguments he uses against his supposedly more radical enemies, the one that remains in some ways most interesting is that about the character of faith itself. His deservedly famous analysis of perseverance in faith goes a long way to separate faith from an identifiable (positive) state of mind and to assimilate it to the constantly renewed act of trust and acceptance of God's unswerving favour which persists even in what is experienced as near-despair.

Hooker's work has its own risks: the formidable argument against the Puritans can easily be turned into a simple presumption in favour of any historically well-grounded way of doing things in the Church and thus into an apology for failing to think critically enough about the Church's practice. It is a legacy that has not been by any means uniformly healthy for the Anglican Church. The appeal to the priority of divine action could, in isolation, lead to an indifference about the discipline, the visible integrity of the Church, precisely that bland inclusivism which has no ultimate interest in theology at all and which is sometimes presented as an ideal for contemporary faith. But this is perhaps why we need to attend to both Hooker and Tyndale. Tyndale's vivid sense of how the shape and character of God's gift determines how we shall live introduces a critical edge to Hooker's appeal for historically educated patience. Doing justice to both elements of this legacy is no easy business; as any contemporary Anglican will confirm.

IV

Studying the history of the Reformation brings into focus some new dimensions of the basic historical and theological question, 'How is the Church to be defined?' Whereas the patristic period puts the emphases upon inner cohesion and discipline combined with doctrinal precision, the Reformation concerns are more diverse and more nuanced. Both discipline and doctrine, in Protestant eyes, can be distorted into a grounding of the Church in human action and achievement, so both need to be challenged. Yet this at the same time implies a formidably severe doctrinal test applied to what Christians say and do, the test of compatibility with the biblical axiom of justification by faith; and it poses serious questions about church order by the mere fact of subverting existing models of hierarchy and authority, so that issues of discipline cannot be neglected. There is something inescapably precarious about any Protestant resolution of these tensions; but a good Lutheran or Reformed Christian would have to say that such precariousness is appropriate to a life grounded in something other than worldly security. And, as we have seen, the entire question of security and continuity affects Catholic sensibility no less deeply. Out of these turmoils in the collective imagination the 'modern' self begins to come to birth – for good or ill.

But there is one further area of theological concern which needs mentioning here, an area of some significance for the late modern Church. The Reformation represented also a reconfiguring of what was believed about the Church's unity. On the Catholic side, nothing very new was added; but the conviction that communion with the Bishop of Rome now involved a higher degree than ever of visible conformity and central control changed the outward aspect of Catholic Christianity more extensively than many at the time could have realised. In the Middle Ages, the international corporation of clerks had indeed assumed the importance of central authority, a single court of appeal; but this had coexisted with a wide variety of clerical jurisdictions, liturgical uses and so on, never standardised by the papacy. The religious orders, most notably, had offered a widespread model of church life alongside the straightforward territorial powers of bishops and the claims of the parochial system. After the Council of Trent, far greater uniformity was required and enforced.

Ironically the churches of the Reformation, in abandoning monastic life and linking themselves so frequently to civic and national identity, followed suit in presupposing that a unified church was one in which patterns of ministry and congregational life were uniform and territorially based. As for unity across local frontiers, attitudes and theologies varied. As we have seen, Lutherans argued for baptism as the sole determining factor in regard to belonging in the Church; but they also repudiated formal sacramental fellowship with those who held different doctrines about the eucharist. Churches of Calvinist heritage tended to see the details of local church administration as legitimately variable, but assumed both doctrinal unanimity on certain points and a recognisable practice of discipline freely exercised by the Church's leadership. While Lutherans tended to solve the unity question at local level by a theology of the authority of the ruler, Calvinists were readier to look to a sort of 'Protestant International', as it has been called, a loose alliance of churches with the same general style of governance and theology. The Reformed Church of England, despite its apparently Lutheran attitude to the monarch, tended to identify with this latter model of international fellowship (not confederation). Some of the bitter controversies that divided it had to do with the extent to which its discipline and form of ministry were really recognisable to 'the best Reformed churches' abroad.

Up to the English Civil War, even the strongest advocates of government by bishops under the Crown still took for granted that this church was part of an unstructured fellowship of Protestant communities, in which it was at least possible to admit clergy ordained abroad to ministry in the English Church.[27] This attitude did not persist; but its widespread prevalence in the early seventeenth century simply draws our attention to what was and was not seen within the Church of England at this period as essential to sacramental fellowship and unity. There might be, and there were, strong feelings and passionate arguments about the concrete application of authority within a national church, but this did not necessarily dictate a doctrinal account of what was necessary to the unity of the Church Catholic across the world.

This is not to make a polemical point about later debates over ministerial validity or the essential role of the episcopate, only to note the fact that the Church of England, like other Reformed churches of the age, held theological views about the Church's unity that were not those of more recent Anglican generations. And because those views have changed far less among continental Protestants than among Anglicans, the latter may find themselves sometimes rather at sea in ecumenical dialogues with those who do not regard ministerial order in the same way as themselves. Indeed, matters can be further complicated when Lutherans in particular would say that a theological scheme that *does* privilege matters of ministerial order implies just such a compromising of God's freedom and priority as Luther sought to root out. Without some sense of the historical issues on both sides — the nature of the concern over justification on the one side, the recognition of the risks of leaving the Church dependent on alien authorities on the other — the debate is endlessly and fruitlessly stalled.

But as we reflect on the Reformation heritage in this connection, it should be clear that some of our current concepts of unity could do with fresh scrutiny. How far is it true that we (both contemporary Catholics and contemporary non-Catholics) assume an ideal of unity that requires more *structural* connectedness and control than either the medieval Church or the 'Reformed International' took for granted? When we repeat formulae about the need for 'organic' unity today, what is the exact force of the adjective?

The challenge posed by the Reformation era is whether it is

possible to conceive the question about unity and communion in the Church as bound to a witness to the priority of God's act rather than to issues around visible structures. This does not relegate the latter to some sort of non-theological status, nor does it sidestep the importance of Scripture or sacramental events; but it does shift the centre of gravity. If we believe that unity is given by God in baptism, and that any other starting point compromises the unique place of divine initiative, some other questions rearrange themselves. Baptism itself makes no sense except in the context of a robust trinitarian theology – it is the gift of a charismatic identity in Christ, the possibility of entering into Christ's prayer, which is, Scripture tells us, the flowering of an eternal relation with the eternal source, and is enabled in us only by the inbreathing of God. In other words, baptism already encodes the theology elaborated by the doctrinal disputes of the early Church. And the sacrament of the eucharist as the regular renewal of this charismatic identity is again primarily a witness to the divine invitation into the place where Christ stands, into Christ's relation with the Father, opened to us by the paschal event, by his cross and resurrection. A very great deal can be said about the essence of the Church simply in reference to what is understood about baptism and eucharist; to grasp these human actions as necessarily and centrally witnesses to what human beings cannot do, as gifts of new identity and relation, is to see why it is possible to define the unity of the Church *first* in relation to this pattern of corporate activity.

To say this is to allow that membership in Christ's Body is determined by God's invitation; but because the Body of Christ is not an ideal community detached from history, we cannot leave that invitation and the form of our response in mid-air, an abstract and invisible thing. Forms of visible continuity with the concrete incarnate life must be taken seriously as confirming that the invitation we are speaking of is actually the invitation of Jesus Christ, in his ministry, death and resurrection, not some general proclamation of generalised divine good will. Baptism is the gift of *this* identity, the eucharist is *his* table. Only so will the life of the baptised believer have an identifiable shape, a discipline and obedience. So the continuity of faithful reading and exposition of the Bible becomes crucial in defining where and what the Church is. And that concern for continuity is the basis for asking what forms in the Church actually express such historical faithfulness – the issue of 'apostolic' identity and continuity in the community. And here the Reformation era warns us against quick answers – the instant affirmation of the need for exact structural continuity or the instant assumption that such structures are of no concern. We shall perhaps have made some progress if we can come to questions about structural and institutional unity by some such route as this.

We are vulnerable to the assumption that what the Council of Trent sought to secure is self-evidently how a unified Church ought to be. At its best, the theological argument of the Reformers presupposes that churches are recognisable to each other by a minimum of actions visibly performed (the sacraments) and by a *method* of arguing and discerning in which it is clear that what is of decisive importance is the specific initiative of God in Jesus – a method which entails a particular attitude to the Bible as the Spirit-guided carrier of God's freedom in communicating to us. Breaches in visible fellowship may, in such a context, be of varying sorts. When Bonhoeffer declared that the opponents of the Confessing Church in Germany were separating themselves from the Catholic Church as such, he was saying that the acceptance of a racial condition for full membership of Christ's Body was to negate *any* claim to be witnessing to divine freedom.[28] But when Lutheran and Reformed Christians originally broke communion because of their diverging theologies of eucharistic presence, there was a somewhat more provisional air about the nature of this division. We don't know how deep this goes (so we might imagine them saying); it seems to go to the heart of our beliefs about Christ's two natures, yet we continue to argue on the basis of Scripture. We recognise a method; we cannot say that there is no speech in common. And so, historically, the seriousness of this division has been variously understood, and variously reconciled, most dramatically in the Confessing Church itself. Perhaps we should say that circumstance alone teaches us what degree of communion is after all possible – as was hinted at the conclusion of the last chapter.

So a breaking of visible fellowship may or may not reflect a fundamental denial of unity. It is possible to say that if visible fellowship commits me to what another local church says in every respect, I need to dissociate myself in order to speak clearly: the breach in the World Alliance of Reformed Churches between the majority and the Dutch Reformed Church of South Africa in the 1980s is one such case; the current divisions in the Anglican Communion may be another. But this is of a different order from Bonhoeffer's principle, and it is important to recognise this (the DRC's acceptance of apartheid was seen as a *heresy* rather than an apostasy; the German Church struggle was more serious, affecting the Church's liberty to define itself). There may be sinful churches that are not apostate churches, because the common language remains. If we are able to acknowledge a unity that remains in such circumstances, we affirm the crucial element of an authentic identity as Church – that is, the abiding act of God, and the givenness of baptism. Beyond this, we are faced with complex practical questions about how the provisionality of such judgements is expressed, the specific limits of visible fellowship; and these are outside our immediate concern here, though none the less serious for that.

One reason for spending some time on this particular question is that it is possible to find ourselves using definitions and standards of unity and communion that either take for granted (as I have said) an excessively robust and structured view of what counts as unity (a picture indebted to the Council of Trent and those who implemented it) or make unity dependent on visible unanimity. The aspects of church history that we have been examining in this chapter, however, suggest that we should not look for the Church's unity in the present or the future – in present agreement or institutional coherence, or in future negotiated consensus; nor should we look for it in a past golden age.

It is at one level always 'past' — that is, always achieved, because grounded in God's purpose 'before the foundation of the world' — and, for us now, grounded in the history of God's covenant and incarnation. Of course we cannot by this means escape the task of discerning now what positions we have to take up and what possible costs to visible unity may be required; but perhaps we can approach these with less anger and anxiety if we have clearly in view that dimension which is out of our hands and our control, the gratuity of God's call. This at the very least puts a question mark against all divisions short of those that (like the crisis to which Bonhoeffer responds) appear to remove even the possibility of common language.

And the essence of the common language that abides through division is, if Luther and Tyndale are right in this respect, praise. One test for the seriousness of a church division might be whether it makes it impossible to say the psalms together. Our common language is not, after all, primarily a language in which to communicate with each other; it is first a language to speak together to God. As this language is more fully learned, we have more to say to each other; when we are at a loss as to how to speak to each other, we can turn to praise. And part of the Reformation's great legacy to the entire Christian world is the making accessible in contemporary and local language of the Bible's idioms of praise and thanksgiving — directly in transla-tion, indirectly in paraphrase and hymnody. We badly need a theology of hymnody as an anticipation of fully discovered unity: of praise as, in the jargon, an eschatological matter.[29]

Debates about the interpretation of Scripture are regularly at the centre of Christian divisions throughout the centuries. Yet the *fact* of Scripture has remained as a unifying and focal element within and between the churches. Perhaps this is because Scripture has been understood not only as a text that informs and instructs with authority but also as a language to be assimi-lated and spoken. This is obviously the case with psalm and canticle; but in a sense the same is true even of its narratives, in which we are given roles to imagine for ourselves, roles that reconstruct our own relation to and speech with God. To accept and in some degree grasp the mystery proposed for saving belief in the pages of the New Testament is not simply to assent to a description of Jesus but to be enabled to say, in his voice, 'Abba, Father'.

Luther and the other great Reformers read the Bible as a text that could and should recreate human language. They were not original in this; and Augustine's theology of biblical reading and interpretation, as well as the simple routine practice of the Church's liturgy in the Middle Ages (especially in the monasteries), nurtured their vision of what it meant to be a community living by the written Word. But their sense that the gratuity of God's work had been obscured by a Church that had become dangerously like a parallel political reality gave extra energy and urgency to their argument. As we have seen, their response to the complex political challenge of the early modern European world brought its own costs and its own fresh crises. But as inheritors of that extraordinary period of early modernity – at least as decisively important as the Enlightenment – we need to see more clearly why and how the Reformation once again made the Church 'strange' to itself in a way that both revived and radically changed the historic and vitalising question of the Church to itself about its true identity. And what this chapter has tried to suggest is how the understanding of all this may revive and change the question for us.

Chapter 4

HISTORY AND RENEWAL: THE RECORDS OF THE BODY OF CHRIST

I

As has been suggested more than once in earlier chapters, the study of church history suffers endemically from different sorts of misplaced certainty. There is the confidence that the past is really the same as the present – 'the present in fancy dress', as I put it earlier. This allows us to appeal to the past as establishing ways of acting and thinking that need only to be faithfully repeated; or it reduces the past to a deviant version of that timelessly valid and obvious way of acting and thinking that characterises the present. The past is not in any serious way strange. The old chestnut about most immemorial British traditions having been invented in the nineteenth century makes the point: we don't want to have to think too hard about the actual *process* by which things come to be done as they are. And to think about processes here means both to understand that the record of the past is a record of change as well as continuity and to see that the way things presently are is something that itself has *come to be*, not something self-evidently right and final. To challenge this first sort of false confidence is to challenge a thoughtless idolatry of both the traditional and the contemporary.

So we are warned against concluding too quickly that we know what people in the past meant. Superficial correspondence in what's done or said should not mislead us as to the labour needed for understanding. A Christian in fourth-century

Antioch, another in eleventh-century Bremen and another in fifteenth-century Paris may be saying very similar things about certain matters at first sight. But what exactly – for example – the act of Holy Communion meant to each of them, or how they viewed the priesthood or the life of prayer or what we might call the nature of mission would be significantly different. And that is not even to begin on the question of their continuities with 'us' (whoever exactly we are, but assuming for the moment that 'we' are modern Western Christians of a certain level of literacy).

But this immediately brings us to the opposite error. The faith of a past age is *of* its age and we cannot assume that it is or could ever be ours. When we read a theologian, a spiritual writer or even a poet from another era, we are at once in a radically foreign environment; no contemporary argument can be settled with the help of the past, no doctrinal statement from the past can be assumed to be authoritative or transparent to our understanding. Dennis Nineham's study of *Christianity, Mediaeval and Modern* is a substantial and intriguing essay in this sort of historical reading:[1] what must be recorded is the embeddedness in a single historical context of all religious statements, so as to show how they cannot be extracted, abstracted, from this setting in a way that makes them credible outside it. The problems with this approach, simply as a matter of history, are manifold; but it can, in simplified form, become another axiomatic, 'obvious' perspective. Instead of the assumption that we *do* know what earlier ages thought and felt, we now assume that we *don't* and probably can't. Taking up the quite legitimate caution against bridging too easily the gulf between present and past, we now decide that the gulf must be more or less unbridgeable.

What both kinds of misplaced certainty forget is that historical understanding is not something totally unlike any other sort of understanding. Our minds engage with what is other – that is what minds do to be minds at all – and go through processes with which we are all in fact familiar. We are puzzled, attracted, frustrated, repelled, intrigued, driven to questioning our starting points, finding them reinforced, finding them less secure than we thought; we have moments of bewilderment and moments of triumphant grasp. We develop a complex relation that ideally expresses itself in respect and patience; we learn the folly of disengaging when frustrated and the folly of supposing too soon that we understand adequately. We acquire not so much a confidence in our solutions as a capacity to continue, a trust in the process.

The greatest of twentieth-century philosophers warned against having a concept of certainty that regarded it as a single and absolute quality of mind attainable by one set of clearly marked methods. Instead, he argued, we need to look at different sorts of uncertainty and the actual ways we have of dealing with them.[2] It does not help to have a paradigmatic case of being certain which can be treated as the norm for every imaginable issue in dispute. 'Am I sure of this?' is a question that arises in a lot of distinctive contexts; the ways in which we learn to continue, to deal with uncertainties and find sufficient ground for carrying on, are diverse and acquired by involvement in the relevant structures of behaving with their various conventions ('forms of life').

Wittgenstein's reflections on certainty ought to be (but are not all that often) a substantive aid for theologians. Before we ask how certainty is to be guaranteed, we should ask where and how the question, 'Am I sure?' has posed itself. And rather than looking for one unshakeable foundation for one kind of certainty, we need to look at what in fact is done to answer the particular questions and doubts that we face. It is not fanciful here to note the echo of the Reformation disputes we looked at in the last chapter: the ground of all our security is God's choice, God's action, God's self-communication; but to reduce this to one human method of securing unshakeable answers to human questions risks reducing God's grace to a system of human guarantees. The issues raised here will need revisiting later in this chapter. The present point, however, is that a theologically sensitive approach to the history of the Church will necessarily avoid both the distortions outlined earlier and ask itself some questions about true and false certainties in respect of the Christian past. It will, in short, be at one level a routine exercise in human understanding, assuming, as in every conversation, the alternations of difficulty and perception, difference and convergence. What is special about it will be what Christians believe about precisely how and why the past matters for them and the exact nature of the understanding hoped and prayed for – something more than a mere historical empathy, the passing convergence of minds from two or more periods.

Churches have always been 'conserving' communities: that is, they have always been concerned about the past and about whether they were in some sense doing the same thing as the previous generation had done. This has something to do with Christianity's special emphasis upon redemption as an event with a particular location and date: if the all-important change in what is possible for human beings depends entirely on a set of events in *this* time and place and no other, there is a prima facie case for concern about whatever links us to such a particular location. Any human community that has a distinctive structure will, of course, be concerned about how to induct new members into its habits; but the Christian Church has the added concern of making sure those habits are a way of bringing believers truthfully and effectively into the presence of a specific past, the incarnate reality of Jesus. What the Church conserves is seen as important because of this concept of becoming contemporary with Jesus. And, as the first chapter of this book suggested, this 'becoming contemporary' involves an openness to those other believers, past as well as present, in whom Jesus is believed to be active. Mature Christian identity is at home with the past – with diverse aspects of it, in diverse ways, but always as posing the question of relation with Jesus. Without this encounter with Jesus in the days of his flesh and in his life in his corporate Body in history, the believing self remains untouched by transforming grace.

Hence the significance of 'conserving' and of 'handing

on' tradition in its literal sense. A twentieth-century Orthodox theologian described tradition in its full theological meaning as the 'charismatic memory' of the Church,[3] and that is a phrase which captures very vividly the idea of historical memory activated by the Holy Spirit in the Body of Christ as a form of grace. It is not an encounter with any sort of innocent and uninterpreted past, nor a guarantee of completely accurate historical recall; it is not something that makes painstaking research and reconstruction unnecessary or even bad. It is the gift that permits the kind of encounter with the past that allows it to be a transforming gift.

And hence the appropriateness of seeing this memory at work primarily in the community's worship. This is where the primary record of God's self-communication, the Bible, is read, not as a relic of the past but as bearing the present communication of God. This is where, from the earliest days of the Church, martyrs have been commemorated and celebrated, where transformed lives are held up to us. And the language of this event is one that is inevitably and rightly not simply contemporary, but a speech formed by generations of practice; where praise is offered not only in the words that are straightforwardly our own, today's words, but in words used and inherited, psalms, canticles, hymnody. It is ultimately this common practice, this habit of inherited speech and 'charismatic' remembering, that tells us how and why the two false certainties we started with miss the point.

In the preceding chapter, we considered how the practice of common praise, in language that was not owned by any one faction or interest group in the Church, was a visible sign of the unity that is given, not achieved. Something of the same applies to our appropriation of the past. If it is most clearly done in worship, then when we sing canticles, psalms and classical hymnody we express a unity across time as well as a unity in space. When Christians sing corporately, they use an extraordinary repertoire. They repeat songs ascribed to a monarch who lived in the Middle East well before the foundation of Rome; they sing

Why Study the Past?

words and music composed by bishops in Dark Age Gaul and Italy; they use (in English-speaking countries usually rather abbreviated) versions of the songs of Martin Luther, and some of the versified paraphrases of the alleged compositions of the Bronze Age monarch from the Middle East; they shuffle and polish with varying degrees of embarrassment the bourgeois pieties and medieval revivalism of the Victorian era. One of the most evident marks of Christian continuity is, in other words, simply the regular business of literally making our own the rhythms and vocabulary of another age. We don't know in what respect we 'mean' what the original composers meant (what would be involved in meaning *the same as* King David or even the poets of four and five centuries later who used his name?). Yet the words remain possible, and the words make certain things possible for us.

The texts are there, with all their historical difficulty (which is why it is a futile and rather insulting exercise to abridge or improve in the light of what happens to make us comfortable or uncomfortable today); they survive because they are *generative*. They have continued to invite new understanding and have opened up new worlds. They stimulate new questions; and, as the Reformation record shows, they generate questions about their own reading, they generate new levels of critical reading as they come to be read in different and unprecedented contexts. Most of us over a certain age will recognise in our individual experience what it is to read a book at eighteen and then return to it twenty years later; as likely as not, we shall find it very different. Aspects of it will strike us as having passed unnoticed the first time; other aspects we may recognise as having unconsciously shaped our response to many other things. We read it perhaps with a sense of never having read it before, and at the same time as being more familiar than we had realised. The earlier reading has made things possible (including this second reading); the person who first read it is not there any longer, and cannot read a second time as if it were the first, but the person reading it the second time is one who has been changed, imperceptibly it may be, by that first reading. In the life of any individual, a book that is reread several times is one that both establishes itself as an intimate and familiar conversational partner, but which at every reading also conceals and reveals different things, opens different doors.[4]

Books or dramas or music that allow us to mature in their company have a very particular role for us; because they are not exhausted by one reading or hearing, they tell us that there is more to be found, that we have a future with them which we cannot predict or control in full. What I am trying to articulate here is that sense of coming into a distinctive landscape that is given us by certain imaginative works; we know that they demand time if we are to 'inhabit' them properly. And in the context of the Church, this is what is being claimed about the texts of Scripture above all, but also about those further texts in which Scripture is fleshed out – the words and forms of worship, and that peculiar kind of text which is a Christlike life. These are the concrete form taken by God's invitation to grow in his company; they are equally the promise of a future.

It is a point worth pondering. To engage with the Church's past is to see something of the Church's future. If we relate to the past as something that settles everything for us, something whose meaning is utterly and finally plain, it is to treat the texts of the past as closing off history, putting an end to our self-awareness as historical persons involved in unpredictable growth. If we dismiss the past as unintelligible, if we read its texts as closed off from us by their alien setting, we refuse to see how we have ourselves been formed in history; we pretend that history has not yet begun. And in the specifically theological context, we shall on either count be denying that we can *only* grow in company, can only develop because summoned by a word that is not ours. That word is made concrete and immediate for us in the human responses that have constituted the Church's history; all of this has made our present believing selves possible. T. S. Eliot, faced with the glib modern claim that 'we know so much more than our ancestors', riposted, 'Yes; and they are what we know.'[5]

As was said in the first chapter, we must become aware of our hidden debts for who we now are.

'Am I sure?'; 'How do I know this is the same Church?' There are several tempting answers that will effectively deny that human beings have their identity in history and appropriate their salvation in history. What this chapter has been suggesting so far is that there is often a pragmatic answer that has to do with the simple practice of the Church as it hopefully or expectantly returns to the accumulation of past reflection as it worships – most specifically as it worships sacramentally, in a context where 'charismatic memory' is of the essence of the act. To do the same (the eucharistic action, in whatever precise form, but identified as done in obedience to Christ), attending prayerfully to the same Scripture, assimilating the language of praise and reflective celebration from apparently distant contexts in the confidence that the landscape into which we are brought will continue to unfold – this is at least the beginning of an answer about the Church's identity that doesn't pretend history is either over or not yet started. It is an answer that helps us see 'how to continue'; it does not deliver a static resolution, but unfolds the ways in which Christian practice has in fact sustained itself, the ways in which as a matter of fact Christians have worked out something of who they are in appropriating their past. The liturgical context is the primary place for this; but from the encounter with the past in this setting, Christians may find more about how to approach the whole of their history with theological imagination and resource.

II

In the first chapter, we were thinking about the difference it makes to our study of the Christian past if we begin from assumptions about belonging together in the Body of Christ. We shall be looking for the contours of the one divine action that sustains the Church; and we shall give special attention to all in the life of the Church that points us to the priority of that action, to the record of praise and repentance and contemplation that establishes the 'grammar' of the Church's language as responsive, as a following and exploring of something once and for all set before us.

But that one divine action is both a set of historical events and an eternal act, the self-giving of the Son to the Father in the Trinity. For the classical theology of the first Christian centuries, the life of Jesus is in its entirety a working out in time of an eternal relation of adoration and love. Thus to be in the Body of Christ now is to be a 'place' in which Christ offers his prayer to the Father; to recognise another as belonging to the Body is to acknowledge that in them also Christ prays his eternal prayer. To attend in love to another member of the Body is to look and listen for how the prayer of Christ sustains and transfigures that life, so that it becomes a gift for my own growing and maturing.

So the Christian seeking to understand the Christian past as a believer not only as an historian has very specially the task of trying to stand with Christians in an earlier age in their prayer. This should not be misunderstood. It is not that every expression of Christian devotion through the ages is usable and creative now; let alone that contemporary devotion should never seek a voice of its own but always defer to what is inherited. What it is possible to say now with commitment and integrity is most unlikely to be exactly what was said in another era. As we saw a little while back, what was prayed by our forebears is part of what makes possible different ways of praying for us ('they are what we know'). But our awareness of words that are still held in common, acts still performed, helps us read what they said within one context which we all share, the act of the Church as it opens itself to the action of the Christ who is present in his Body.

And part of what this means is that the Christian historian looks not only for the ways in which Christians in the past shared the cultural assumptions of their day but for what in that complex of belief and action held open the possibility of change. It is relatively easy to write about how Christians in the patristic period shared the general contemporary attitudes;[6] we are thoroughly familiar with the almost unrelieved landscape of theological misogyny across great desert tracts of the Church's record. Yet the cultures formed by Christianity came to find slavery intolerable and to affirm the equality of women. Christians slowly came to think of whatever it was that supported slavery and misogyny in their tradition as an alien growth. When we examine a past period, we should, then, ask what it was that made it impossible for Christians simply to repeat what had been said; we should look for what was not simply the reflection of cultural attitudes.

A theological history is alert for something irreducible to a mere cultural setting;[7] if it is looking out for signs of the act of God in the Church, it will be looking in each period for what unsettles the Church, what appears with increasing urgency as unfinished business. In the third chapter, we looked briefly at how the late medieval period inexorably moved towards a situation where certain questions could no longer be evaded. When they are finally confronted, it is with a confidence that something in the tradition itself will provide the life and energy to remould the Church's present life.

The dangers of looking to the past for a solution of present difficulties are obvious enough; but there is another way of approaching this which is less fraught with risk. If we begin from our axiom of common membership in the Body, there will always be gifts to be received from the past; we can expect that we shall find something that we had not grasped until a contemporary crisis had brought it into focus. Hence the extraordinary regularity with which radical renewal in the Church has come from a new appropriation of tradition of one sort or another. The Reformation is an obvious case, but the twentieth century offers some dramatic instances as well. If we look at the three great confessional traditions of Orthodoxy, Roman Catholicism and Protestantism between the thirties and the fifties of the last century, it is clear that the movements of greatest theological vitality are all movements of 'recovery', *ressourcement*, rather than simple innovation or simple repetition. In the Orthodox world, the new readings of the Greek Fathers by Russian theologians in particular generated a fresh approach to the theology of the human person and the nature of communion and community which continues to have remarkable impact on ecumenical work. In the Roman Catholic Church, we have first the rediscovery of the potential of Aquinas by figures like Jacques Maritain, in revolt against textbook scholasticism;[8] and then the 'new theology' of the post-war period, in which scholasticism itself was challenged by a retrieval of the same Greek Fathers.[9] The foremost Protestant theologian of the age, Karl Barth, abandoned the most fashionable and accessible intellectual models of theological modernity to think through afresh the themes of Paul, Anselm, Kierkegaard and Calvin, as the most relevant and critical contribution possible to the unprecedented disasters of twentieth-century Germany.

None of these figures and movements has fared well at the hands of more strictly professional historians of ideas. In their somewhat chilly light, it is obvious that the Greek Fathers read by Russian theologians such as Vladimir Lossky and Georges Florovsky were being absorbed through a medium of sub-Hegelian philosophy as reworked by the idiosyncratic religious philosophers of Russia's 'Silver Age' before the First World War – philosophers violently repudiated by the new theologians.[10] Maritain's version of Thomas Aquinas owes a fair amount to Maurice Blondel and, even if only by reaction, to Henri Bergson, as well as to a particular reading of Aquinas in the sixteenth century.[11] The post-war Catholic recovery of the Fathers would also have been very different without Blondel – but it would have been different too without the immediacy of the challenge of existentialism. Barth's Anselm, Barth's Calvin, even Barth's St Paul, owe a lot to Barth's Kierkegaard; and Barth's brilliant reinterpretation of Calvinist doctrine about predestination is clearly advancing a vision Calvin could not have owned.

But once again we have to appeal to the question of how certain things are made possible. When Vladimir Lossky read the Greek Fathers, he read — of course — with centuries of European intellectual history in his mind and, more specifically, with the heritage of his own Russian forebears (although he was so powerfully critical of it in many ways).[12] But he also posed the perfectly fair question of where some currents in all that find their origin. By worrying at the logic of trinitarian theology in the fourth century, he was able to conclude that the very notion of a distinctive spiritual identity that could not be reduced to a set of shared characteristics, generic elements of a common essence, could only come into focus in the course of the search for adequate intellectual tools to deal with revelation. Christian faith demands that we find a way of speaking about God as more than an individual possessed of divine nature, yet without falling into the mythological trap of supposing several divine individuals. What slowly and haltingly emerges is a sense of divine plurality as an interrelation of subsistent actions, each distinguished by its relation to the others, each existing as an act of self-bestowal, self-emptying, a going-out from individuality into identity in and with the other. The innately mysterious character of distinctive personal identity thus imagined is something that has to be thought through in relation to humanity as well as divinity, since human beings are in God's image. And so we come to the position that human personal being has about it something of the utter resistance to category and species-being that we see in the interrelating life of God. The persons of the Trinity are not projections of human individuality (that would be to believe in three gods); it is rather that human individuality is a fractured picture of divine personal being. The more we leave behind the idea of a self as one among many centres from which a set of repeatable attributes is exercised, the more we move to understand our selfhood as fulfilled only in self-forgetful relation, the more we realise the divine image which is the fundamental potential of our humanity.[13]

Lossky is making a twofold claim. First, very simply, he is arguing that without the painful struggle to find words for the revealed mystery of the Trinity we should not have the words to do adequate justice to the depths of human dignity and the frightening scale of human vocation. We should not have the elusive, exhilarating, complex idea of a distinctiveness that is more than individuality, the idea of a sort of inexhaustibility in every human subject. Second, he is suggesting that the doctrine of the Trinity as developed in the fourth century leaves a trail, as we might say: what is said about God inevitably impacts, sooner or later, on what we say about humanity, given the other doctrinal positions of Christian faith (creation and incarnation).

Now a scholarly analysis of the fourth-century Fathers appealed to by Lossky is likely to produce a far more confused and perhaps less inspiring result. The conceptual inconsistencies of the Fathers will be made plain; the distance between what they thought about human beings and what 'we' moderns think will be apparent. It is fair to raise some serious questions when something like Lossky's theology is simply put forward as 'the teaching of the Fathers'. Yet I should want to argue that a great deal of what Lossky says remains unaffected by the plain investigation of what the fourth-century writers 'actually' meant. He is claiming that they do, as a matter of fact, move the theological discussion on and allow things to be said that could not be said before; and, as a theologian rather than just an intellectual historian, he assumes that new language about God will naturally affect the self-understanding of humans. As a modern, with modern interests in the definition of the personal, interests in human dignity or liberty, Lossky is inevitably faced with the challenge of connecting these concerns to his own doctrinal heritage. His response is to say that precisely these 'modern' interests are the long-term effect of a shift in theological language sixteen hundred years ago. The weight and seriousness of these interests is a mark of their origin in reflection on the most fundamental issues there could be. And the challenge of the way in which such concerns are spoken of today is best met by the creative archaeology that traces them to their proper origin.

Something similar is evidently at work in Catholic retrievals of Aquinas: how better to identify with the modern protest against static views of human identity than by recovering what Thomas says about the act of being – being as such considered as unimpeded action, with finite beings stimulated into action according to their innate levels of responsiveness to the foundational movement of infinite being?[14] Or, in the context of the Catholic patristic revival, how better to challenge the potentially stultifying idea that God's purposes for creation are essentially disconnected from the 'natural' purposes of things (and persons) than by reviving the Greek patristic conviction that creation is made to be open to God's future, and is only itself as and when it grows into this?[15]

Henri de Lubac, one of the greatest expositors of this new approach to the writings of the Fathers, summed up the situation very accurately in his *Paradoxes of Faith*:

> In the face of documents taking us back to the origins of our Faith, two attitudes confront one another, equally indispensable.
>
> The critic must always be afraid of overcharging the texts, of 'making them say more than they do', of letting himself be affected unintentionally by all that has been subsequently got out of them. The religious man, on the other hand, dreads not understanding them in their fulness. The former must shun what is arbitrary; the latter does not want to stay on the surface.[16]

To approach the texts of our history trying to avoid either distorting or patronising is not easy. And we are brought back here to some of the very basic issues with which this investigation began. We are liable to erode the real difference between present and past, ignoring what makes the past genuinely strange to us; we are equally liable to treat the past simply as a set of inadequate attempts to think or do what we now know how to think and do. But a theologically intelligent reading of our history requires something more serious. For a grasp of real difference as well as real continuity, we need what de Lubac calls the critic; we need to allow critical scholarship to suspect and turn inside out what is before us, to do its worst; but we cannot lose sight of the fact that, if this history is indeed ours, to examine it is to examine our own identity.

For the believer, the governing principle is, we might say, that of *analogy*. We read our past confident that there is a reality to which we relate in common, something that is realised diversely in irreducibly different contexts; as has already been spelled out, this reality is our relation with God in Christ. And, as with every analogy in all intellectual fields, to reduce the difference is to weaken the necessary tension in the principle. I noted in the first chapter the temptation to look for a period of Christian history in which the ordinary ambiguities or corruptions of human history have not obscured the truth of the gospel – a primitive egalitarian Church, a harmonious medieval synthesis, an Anglican Golden Age before the Civil War. In the modern era, there has been a repeated tendency to look to the culturally marginal areas of the Church for inspiration. Celtic Christianity and Syrian Christianity have both served as a foil to the Roman or Byzantine 'mainstream'. The former in particular continues to be regarded in many quarters as a model of creation-affirming, community-building, non-hierarchical faith which offers an alternative to 'Augustinian' or 'Roman' doctrine and practice. It is reinforced sometimes by a fanciful reading of Pelagius (positive attitudes to creation because there is no such thing as original sin), sometimes by an equally fanciful understanding of ancient Celtic religion (in a way that would have much surprised those Welsh and Irish saints who threw down pagan altars with as much enthusiasm as any 'Roman').[17]

This is not pure nonsense or waste; a really constructive engagement with forms of faith that are outside the supposed mainstream is one of the most important critical resources we can bring to a mature understanding of the Church. But it becomes dangerous and stultifying if we make any part of the past a mirror for our own preferences and assumptions. We may look back here to a point made in the first chapter and open it up in a little more detail. There are communities and groups in the past whose voices were undoubtedly suppressed by an anxious and often unscrupulous hierarchy – women, Gnostics, Celts, if you will; but that they were suppressed does not mean that they were suppressed for believing what we believe. Simply because we have varying levels of unease about what the 'mainstream' Church has concluded does not entitle us to think that all those who disagreed with them agree with us. Gnostics attacked episcopal hierarchy and biblical literalism; various groups of them also argued for inflexible predestined divisions between classes of humans, or for the evil of the flesh and the female. Whatever we may want to say about them, we need to be cautious about regarding them as forerunners of a liberal and enlightened faith fitted for the contemporary market. Celtic Christians disagreed with aspects of centralised Church authority – but not as regards ethics or doctrine or even vernacular liturgy; and a glance at the Irish penitentials should disabuse anyone of the notion that Celtic Christians were instinctively hostile to legalism. Pelagius opposed the theology of original sin, but argued in consequence an unmitigated duty to obey the moral law by our efforts and the most stringent sanctions for disobedience.[18] If we are to learn from any such suppressed or disadvantaged voices, we must first let them be themselves; they are at least as strange as any 'orthodox' voices from the past.

Recognising and developing analogy is a matter of allowing the historical other to be other (if we did not, we should be turning our backs on the very idea of real change in time), but then exploring our actual or potential indebtedness to that other, its role in shaping our own world and our own possibilities. That analogy is, for the Christian, grounded finally in Christ – in the belief that one action is going on in the Body of Christ, one prayer being prayed. And in the light of that belief, we have good reason for not trying to minimise the strangeness of the Church's past; only if we depend on facile and immediately demonstrable continuities of feeling and expression is this a problem. But if we assume a unity which depends on the given presence of Christ, the strangest and most apparently unpromising aspects of our past may speak to us unexpectedly – not in a way that removes their difficulty, sometimes their real obnoxiousness, but as enlarging our awareness of Christ, whose work is not confined to a narrow range of those persons and settings we find congenial.

In the last analysis, there is a sort of reciprocity at work here between our beliefs about Christ and our attitude to the historical Body of Christ. The conviction of Christ's status as divine allows us to see the possibility of identifying his presence in an unlimited variety of human lives associated with his by faith; and the continuing activity of so 'reading' human lives and finding Christ fills out practically the belief in his identity as more than an historical individual of the past. The more we look at and listen to the variety of the Christian past, the more we grasp something of the scope of that which makes the Christian record possible, that to which all Christian thinking and acting is a response.

III

Some of what we have just been thinking about opens up the question of *authority* in the Church – not so much the actual executive structures of the community as the criteria to which appeal can be made in identifying the boundaries of what counts as Christian. Over the centuries, as we have seen, history itself has been quarried in various ways so as to answer the question. For Eusebius in the fourth century the doctrine uninterruptedly taught in the great urban churches of the Mediterranean by acceptably spiritual leaders and teachers was the standard by which innovation could be measured; a method that did not serve him well at the Council of Nicaea. For some Reformed apologists in the sixteenth century, there was a watershed in the Church's story before which all was relatively well: John Jewel, Bishop of Salisbury, the most distinguished defender of the Reformed Church of England in the early part of Elizabeth I's reign, appealed to the first six hundred years of Christianity.[19]

Others were less precise, but agreed in considering that there had been an early period that could act as a touchstone in controversy.

It should be reasonably clear that this in itself is not an answer to anxieties about authority. There are too many problems in delimiting the golden age, too many bits of special pleading that have to be entered when the evidence for primitive purity is less than compelling. The whole idea that there is a *privileged* era for being a Christian is a strange one. Kierkegaard argued passionately that there was and could be no advantage for the believer in happening to be contemporary with the first witnesses of faith; this would make belief itself depend in some way on the chances of time.[20] If we say that the Bible is the touchstone for authoritative teaching, this cannot be taken to mean that all we need to do in order to arrive at orthodox faith is to reconstruct what was going on in the minds of the human authors of Scripture. Yet we cannot be Christians without the Bible or without the history of its reading, and we constantly look in this direction for some kind of resolution of our debates and uncertainties.

One line of response that has emerged in these pages might be put in this way, playing a little with the roots of the word 'authority'. The question is about the 'authorship' of who and what we are: authority in the Church's teaching is bound up with what makes the Church's situation here and now open to its authorship in the act of God. Confronted with dispute or controversial novelty, the sort of question that the believer needs to consider is how far a particular option in the debate or a particular innovation tends to obscure the transparency of the Church to God's action. A claim that any new practice or teaching can be held without weakening this transparency needs to establish itself by demonstrating how it refers to or opens out upon the confession of divine priority, how it can be related to the divine authorship of the community of belief. Hence the crucial importance of argument on the basis of the most universal common language, that of the Bible; but hence too the importance of having a theologically alert approach to the past of the Church, to the way in which questions about the essence of the Church are raised in the debates of past centuries.

Let me take two examples, both of them with some resonance in the contemporary ecclesiastical scene. First, there is manifest and heated controversy in parts of the Anglican Church over the possibility of licensed lay people presiding at the celebration of the eucharist; and the practice already exists in some other communions, variously restricted and controlled. The idea is defended on a number of grounds, all of them theologically serious. It is a matter on which Scripture as such appears to give no direct guidance; it is a response to pastoral need; it is a way of affirming the wholeness of the Christian community's subsistence in every congregation gathered for worship (and so requiring no importation of an ordained person to complete or guarantee its viability as a eucharistic assembly).[21]

How does the idea relate to the basic theology of the Church's 'authorship' in God's act? The defender will argue that it is at the very least a matter of indifference in this context; given the silence of scriptural witness, nothing essential can hang upon it. To the extent that it decisively repudiates a particular theology of ordained ministry that is positively anti-scriptural (the idea of a special caste of Christians with distinctive supernatural powers), it could be said to reinforce a sound theology of the Church. In denying that a faithful congregation needs this specific kind of hierarchical or structural guarantee of its authenticity, it emphasises the free summons of God's word to the congregation over any human institutional considerations.

The critic might respond by underlining the theological risk of giving such prominence to the local congregation without spelling out what makes it organically united with the Church Catholic. Our indebtedness for our Christian identity to other Christians now and other Christians in the past is a central aspect of believing that the Church is Christ's Body, not a transient human association. The requirement that the eucharist is celebrated by an ordained minister is not about the powers of the ministry but about the catholicity of the congregation, its proper openness and recognisability to the wider Church, so that the eucharist is more than the prayer of this group alone. A more detailed response would fill this out by saying that this 'more than' directs us to the sacrificial self-offering of Christ to the Father, into whose movement we are drawn in our 'sacrifice' of praise and thanksgiving. Without some means of identifying this local action with the act of the whole Church and of Christ in his whole Body, we weaken (fatally?) the model of the Church as a network of mutual dependence and mutual acknowledgement. It may be that in the abstract there could be other ways of signifying this than the ordained minister at the Table; but as a matter of fact, this is the 'grammar' of recognisability that has established itself (not only in episcopally ordered churches).

There are of course further counter-claims that could and should be heard from the advocates of a change in practice; but my purpose has been to show how a theological argument on these issues can be sketched, with an appeal on both sides to the principle of transparency to God's action. Even in a case where scriptural evidence is not decisive, there is the possibility of an appeal to the criterion of conformity with the act of revelation. Where there is more obvious scriptural material to invoke on one side or the other (as in debates about divorce, women's ministry or homosexual activity), the challenge to a programme of innovation is to show that a desired change, in subordinating one aspect of the biblical text to another, or arguing for a re-evaluation of a whole complex of texts, is not weakening the fundamental commitment to the Church's foundation in initiative and gift from elsewhere. Hence some of the frustrations in these debates: some who argue for innovation are frustrated because it is invariably assumed by opponents that they argue only from current social attitudes; some who defend existing convention are no less frustrated because their views are assumed to be rationalisations of prejudice or reaction. All of this would be less unedifying if – as we noted in the second chapter – we were better able to identify the criteria for recognising theological argument as such, and better able to connect specific issues with the underlying concerns about the integrity of the Church itself.

But now to the second issue which may help to illustrate the method of argument. The Church's involvement in interfaith dialogue in the last quarter of the twentieth century has inevitably raised questions about boundaries in practice: is it ever right to take part in interfaith acts of worship? It seems fairly obvious at first that this poses a problem for the Christian: if Christian worship is the act of Christ in his Body, it is not simply a human activity whose context and object can be left vague. To worship in words shared with non-Christians is to suggest that worship is an activity *we* are somehow in charge of; it happens when and how we decide.

Now if there is a case for interfaith worship on theological grounds, it would have to be made out in terms that showed it to be a proper expression of transparency to the initiative of God in the Church; it would have to be shown to *be* an action of the Church, in fact. This is not easy. But a skilful theologian might argue that the action of praying in Christ to the Father is something that is 'given' to the baptised person in such a way that *this* is always what happens when they dispose themselves for personal or corporate prayer; and that to require the language used always to be explicit about this is to draw attention away from the givenness of the relation with the praying Christ. To be alongside others of other religious confessions in an act of worship doesn't nullify the fact of being in Christ: the Church is, and is active in Christ, wherever baptised people are; and nothing is compromised by finding words on occasion to share with those who don't share baptism.

I am less than convinced by this, I admit; it is really no more than a guess at what sort of argument in defence of interfaith worship would go any way to satisfy the sort of criteria I have been proposing – to see, that is, if a really theological argument could be had about this, rather than just assuming the question was not discussable. I think that, ultimately, the separation of two elements here, an inner relatedness to Christ and an outer flexibility about words and forms, takes away something vital from the idea that God calls into being a tangible human community, whose common language is the carrier of its common relatedness to Christ's invitation. Move away from this, and the visible reality of the Church becomes something almost optional, in a way that makes more abstract the interdependence of believers on one another – their interdependence precisely as visible, material, historical and language-using subjects.

I must add that it seems to me axiomatic that there will be important, creative convergences of language in interfaith dialogue. As has so often been said in recent years, Jewish, Christian and Muslim vocabulary for God has many common roots, and the sympathetic hearing of each other's speech for and to God is a matter of spiritual deepening and intellectual enrichment.[22] Further afield, Christian–Buddhist dialogue has discovered other sorts of shared depths.[23] But to listen to each other means listening to the language that expresses distinct identities; for Christians to be listened to means that they have to speak from the position of the baptised. It is possible to stand silently together, possible to welcome someone of another faith into an act of worship in your own community, possible to be welcomed in another community. But the integrity of the act of worship itself – for Christian and non-Christian alike – needs to be affirmed as a locus of authority and transparency, I should want to argue. The attempt to find a non-committal language for a shared act of worship still seems to draw us away from the central conviction of Christians that they are enabled to recognise in each other one activity across the boundaries of time and cultural difference. The kind of recognition that so importantly happens in interfaith encounter, when the Christian senses something of Christ's agency in another, can only fully be *celebrated* when there is some common self-understanding (otherwise it may lead to a presumptuous short-circuiting of the other's real and continuing otherness).

These unavoidably brief and inadequate discussions are an

attempt to show how the historically grounded sense of theology as about the fundamental distinctiveness of the Christian community at worship can help us to avoid the depressingly familiar sort of church debate that does not begin to clarify what might be common criteria, what all participants would agree counts as an argument. These pages have been trying, in other words, to put forward a way of engaging with the Christian past that is constructive for Christians as such: church history as a spiritual discipline, not only a critical or scientific one. As I have stressed, it will not be a spiritual one if it is not also critical; the development of some techniques of scientific history has been a good and welcome dissolving agent for self-serving, propagandist versions of the past. But to stop with this is to isolate ourselves as contemporary believers from the unceasing conversation of the Body of Christ in time. Whether we use the past as an inflexible standard of correctness or neglect it as a record of premodern error, we isolate ourselves from the real life of the past. And when the past in question is that of the Church, that real life is in its ultimate depth the life of Christ.

IV

Spiritual disciplines are invariably methods of challenging the assumption that I – my conscious, willing ego – stand at the centre of all patterns of meaning. Silence, fasting, receiving the sacraments, confession and penance, even listening to a sermon, have all been listed as spiritual disciplines because they all direct themselves to this 'decentring' exercise, without which, the Christian believes, the impact of the true God upon us will always be muted, perhaps stifled, by our own scripts and dramas. Throughout this discussion of the Christian past, the theme of 'decentring' has been significant. In the first chapter, we noted the difficulty of accepting the fact that our current consciousness and our current identity are made – the fruit of interactions that are not measurable. Throughout, there has been an emphasis upon the way in which we are drawn back to a fundamental question about the Church's character as a community that has been convoked or convened by an act independent of itself; so that we are all, in the Church, living 'in the wake' of something prior to all our thoughts and initiatives. The early Church expresses this in martyrdom, the final acknowledgement that our lives are not our own to make over to some human tyranny. The Reformation debates are an angry and passionate quarrel over how to embody the conviction of God's priority without betraying the real responsibility of creatures in time to find language and order in which to communicate. And the whole record of the Church's struggle to find its proper definition gives us some perspective on the vexed question of authority in the Church: how do we live and act as if we were serious about our accountability to the prior act of God?

The sense of the alienness and difficulty of the past should reinforce for the believer the sense of astonishment at the range of human expression and experience that can be counted as Christian, and so fill out the doctrinal conviction that the work of Christ is capable of translation into every human context of culture and imagination. The sense of continuity reinforces the acknowledgement, not always welcome in our own cultural environment, that what we have found it possible to say is what we have learned, what we have been taught, what others have made possible for us. We recognise ourselves and our concerns in a 'distant mirror' (borrowing the title of a famous book on the late Middle Ages),[24] and so are reminded that we are not our own authors, that we have not *just* discovered what it is to be human, let alone what it is to be Christian. And all this has the important consequence that, if we are free to listen to the strange and recognisable 'otherness' of the past, this may help us in dealing with what is strange to us now. An attitude of mind that is not capable of engaging in recognition with the past of the Church is also one that is likely to be closed off from what is different or challenging in the present.

Christians these days are not finding it easy to debate across cultures. Whether it is the liberal–conservative standoff within many of the Western churches, or the difficult dialogues between Western and Eastern churches, or the diverse priorities of churches in the developing world and those of the prosperous global 'north', the problems are often similar. Coping with these challenges is a good deal harder if we have no discipline of questioning our starting points, if we are wedded to assumptions about the obviousness of where we stand. To engage seriously with the Church's history in its strangeness is one way in which such questioning arises. All serious study, it has been said, is a kind of dispossession; difficulty is a moral matter, something that refuses us the comfort we crave. Bishop Westcott, reflecting in the nineteenth century on the problems of biblical interpretation,[25] said that God had revealed himself in such a way as not to spare us *labour*; God speaks in a manner that insists we continue to grow in order to hear (an echo of Augustine in the *Confessions* imagining God urging us to 'Grow and feed upon me').[26] So much of our debate can actually be an evasion of labour. And accepting the labour of having to live with a history that insists upon our involvement is one of the challenges of believing not only in a revealed religion but in one that sees each of us as indebted to all. If it isn't an option simply to discard our history, we are bound to this demanding conversation, this mutual questioning of past and present, in which we discover more fully what we are as a community and who we are as baptised Christians. Out of this, we hope, comes a more mature skill in listening and conversing now.

It is no accident that a culture such as ours, which is alarmed by challenges to its self-evident superiority, is confused about the past, in some of the ways outlined in our first chapter.[27] And it is a major irony that a culture determined to affirm diversity is so poorly equipped to understand the difference embodied in its own history, the distance between past ages and ours. Western modernity, of course, has had to struggle for decades with successive challenges to its natural superiority. For a great deal of the twentieth century, it confronted a philosophy which insisted upon a single direction to history, a secular scheme, but one that organised history into a unity as compelling as any religious vision. With the recession of Marxism, the Western world now faces an increasingly articulate and critical religious system which denies the possibility of rational social organisation independent of revelation. Confronted with Islam, Western modernity has yet to find a mode of engagement that allows for real self-criticism; it seems almost impossible to grant that the new universal story of globalised communication and economic control and interaction does not inevitably lead to accepting the story of Western modernity's rational and universal triumph.

And it is in part this situation which should urge Christians to tackle with more energy and skill their own share in the history of 'the West'. Christian history is part of modernity's buried and frequently denied biography. To disinter some of this biography is not only something that makes for the health of the Church; it is a seriously needed contribution to the intellectual and emotional well-being of the culture.[28] A Church that shares the widespread and fashionable illiteracy of this culture about how religious faith worked in other ages is grossly weakened in its witness. That witness has to do with a promise of universal community that is grounded not in assumptions about universal right and reason but in a narrative displaying how communication is made possible between strangers by a common relatedness to God's presence and act in history – in an historical person. Trying to understand – and to celebrate – the full diversity of Christian history as the record of one community is also to offer to the world we are in a model of life together that does not depend on cultural homogeneity. Christian history shows how believers have constantly, if not reinvented the Church, then at least rediscovered and redefined its essence. The labour of telling the story of all this has always involved the difficult business of identifying what gives continuity or unity across major divisions; in an age of tougher and more sceptical historical tools, that labour is in many ways greater, but the lessons to be learned are correspondingly more interesting and more far-reaching as we try to make sense of Christian identity now. If the historical strangers we celebrate and converse with are stranger than we first thought, that underlines the strangeness of the very fact of the Church, of our belief in the Body of Christ. And this strengthens the conviction that the appropriate response to the fact of the Church is gratitude. A Church that reflects more systematically on why it should be grateful for its existence is a more effective witness to revelation than one that has ceased to be surprised by itself. And in a world caught between chaotic diversity and some very malign versions of global unity, the acknowledgement that human community is both a gift and a surprising gift can bring a welcome touch of reality to what often seems a deeply confused set of aspirations for global harmony.

The God whose identity is enacted in the history of Jesus and followed, explored and articulated in the Church's history is a God who cannot be reduced to the level of an agent within history among others. This God is, in other words, a stranger in the most radical way possible. Yet the story that is told is of a God who wills to be in communion with human agents in all times and all corners of the world. Christian theology celebrates a divine stranger who creates a common world; and in so doing it establishes once and for all the possibility of a humanity that does not depend for its harmony on any transient human alliances or definitions of common interest or common purpose. If our exploration of the Church's history can bring alive the full challenge that this poses to religious and secular tribalism, it will be more than worthwhile. If it can contribute to a certain conversational humility in our garrulous and unself-critical culture, to a better awareness of the labour involved in historical self-understanding, it will have opened a few windows in what can be a dangerously stifling environment. It will have shown a little of what Christians have meant by allying their freedom with the alien sovereignty of God.

NOTES

Chapter 1: MAKING HISTORY: WHAT DO WE EXPECT FROM THE PAST?

1. On the whole question of chronicles and their assumptions, there are some illuminating remarks in Hayden White, 'The Value of Narrativity in the Representation of Reality', *On Narrative*, W. J. T. Mitchell (ed.), University of Chicago Press, 1981, pp. 1–232, especially pp. 7–11.

2. As will, I hope, be clear later on, this does not mean that historical detachment is impossible or illusory. Richard J. Evans, *In Defence of History*, London, Granta Books, 1997, ch. 7, discusses the balance in writing history between the specific and political interests inevitably represented by the historian and the need for critical distance. See in particular pp. 211 ff. on the limits of claiming that all history is identity-building.

3. Norman Davies, *The Isles. A History*, 2nd edn, London, Macmillan, 2000. Ch. 6, 'The Isles of *Outremer*', argues brilliantly for the marginality of British concerns to the Plantagenets, inviting us to rethink this dynasty as a French clan with extensive but not all-important English properties.

4. Michel de Certeau, *L'étranger, ou l'union dans la différence*, Paris, Desclée de Brouwer, 1991, p. 105.

5. Henri de Lubac, *Paradoxes of Faith,* San Francisco, Ignatius Press, 1987, p. 145. c.f. p. 98 on 'the judgement of history' – 'But history too will be judged'.

6. For a readable and sophisticated summary, see Thomas L. Thompson, *The Bible in History. How Writers Create a Past*, London, Jonathan Cape, 1999. For critical responses, see for example V. Philips Long, D. W. Baker and G. J. Wenham, *Windows into Old Testament History*, Grand Rapids, Eerdmans, 2002.

7. See R. Williams, 'Defining Heresy', in *The Origins of Christendom in the West*, Alan Kreider (ed.), Edinburgh, T. & T. Clark, 2001, pp. 313–35.

8. See the remarks of Irenaeus of Lyons in his *Adversus haereses*, I.31.1–2; on this subject, there is scholarly discussion by Birger Pearson, 'Cain and the Cainites', *Gnosticism, Judaism and Early Christianity*, Birger Pearson (ed.), Minneapolis, Fortress Press, 1990, pp. 95–107, and in Alastair Logan, *Gnostic Truth and Christian Heresy,* Edinburgh, T. & T. Clark, 1996, especially ch. 6. For some cautions about assuming too readily that there was a standard and consistent convention of reversing the values in a biblical text – while accepting the evidence for some such intepretation – see M. A. Williams,

Rethinking 'Gnosticism'. An Argument for Dismantling a Dubious Category, Princeton University Press, 1996, pp. 62–79.

9. For the celebrated controversy between Creighton and Acton, see Louise Creighton, *Life and Letters of Mandell Creighton,* London, Longmans, Green & Co., 1906, vol. 1, pp. 368–76. Crieghton, in a letter to a friend, observes that Acton 'demands that history should be primarily a branch of the moral sciences, and should aim at proving the immutable righteousness of the ideas of modern Liberalism'. In contrast, 'I try ... to see their limitations, and leave the course of events to pronounce the verdict upon system and men alike' (p. 376). To Acton himself, he says (p. 369): 'What they [sc. past agents] did was not always what they tried to do, or thought that they were doing.' It is clear that Creighton believed that there were indeed objective moral judgements to be passed, and objective accounts of what was 'really' going on in a past situation, but that the historian had to deal with the level of what those agents themselves experienced as possible or intelligible.

10. On the evolution of Eusebius's work see Timothy Barnes, *Constantine and Eusebius,* Harvard University Press, 1981, section 2; on Eusebius' leading themes, see Robert M. Grant, *Eusebius as Church Historian,* Oxford, Clarendon Press, 1980.

11. See R. Williams, '*Damnosa haereditas*: Pamphilus' Apology and the Reputation of Origen', in *Logos. Festschrift für Luise Abramowski,* H. C. Brennecke (ed.), E. L. Grasmuck and C. Markschies, Berlin, Walter de Gruyter, 1993, pp. 151–69.

12. The *Panegyric to Constantine* was delivered on the occasion of the emperor's thirtieth anniversary in office and is often referred to as the 'tricennial' oration. See Barnes, *op. cit.,* pp. 253–5. For a convenient translation of some key passages, see *Documents in Early Christian Thought,* Maurice Wiles and Mark Santer (eds.), Cambridge University Press, pp. 230–4.

13. Saeculum. *History and Society in the Theology of St Augustine,* Cambridge University Press, 2nd edn, 1970.

14. Augustine, *The City of God,* xiv.27, for the classic summary of this contrast between the two 'cities'.

15. The last chapter of Bede's *Ecclesiastical History of the English People* (V.xxiii) gives an overview of the state of 'Britannia', listing the bishops and some of the monarchs of the areas acknowledging Roman discipline, and ending with an implicit warning against the too eager abandonment of martial skills, which might be needed to repulse the 'British', although these are for the moment largely subject to the 'English'. On these questions, see N. P. Brooks, 'Canterbury, Rome and the Construction of English Identity', in J. Smith (ed.), *Early Mediaeval Rome and the Christian West,* Leiden, Brill, 2000, and, on Bede's method in general, W. Goffart, *The Narrators of Barbarian History,* Princeton University Press, 1988.

16. *Ecclesiastical History* I.xiv and xxii on the corruption of the British before and after the Germanic incursions and their failure to preach the faith to the

newcomers, II.ii on the British refusal to accept Augustine's authority and the consequent punishment.

17. Gildas wrote his treatise *On the Downfall of Britain* some time around 540. It deals with the events following the Roman departure and the moral corruption of several western British principalities and their rulers, and is a significant source for Bede.

18. Henry Chadwick's comprehensive study, *East and West. The Making of a Rift in the Church: From Apostolic Times until the Council of Florence,* Oxford University Press, 2003, shows abundantly how the making of controversial dossiers on both sides of a debate could paralyse any substantial engagement with the underlying theological issues.

19. See Patrick Collinson's essay, 'Truth and Legend: The Veracity of John Foxe's Book of Martyrs', in his *Elizabethan Essays,* London/Rio Grande, Hambledon Press, 1994, pp. 151–77.

20. For a very instructive and original overview of the engagement of the Protestant Reformation with patristic tradition, see ch. 6, 'Scripture and Tradition in the Reformation' in D. H. Williams, *Retrieving the Tradition and Renewing Evangelicalism,* Grand Rapids, Eerdmans, 1999.

21. The new techniques of printing united happily with controversial enthusiasm; the mid-sixteenth century was a golden age of first printed editions of the Fathers. And since this often involved the printing of hitherto virtually unknown manuscript material, existing in very few copies, there could be surprises in the course of debate. The noted Protestant Peter Martyr Vermigli, debating in Oxford with Catholic scholars in 1549, was able to cause some embarrassment by referring to texts of the fifth-century Theodoret of Cyrrhus printed two years earlier in Rome but unknown to his opponents.

22. The Centuriators of Magdeburg were the authors of a *Historia Ecclesiae Christi,* published between 1559 and 1574, arguing a fiercely Protestant case against the corruption of primitive faith by papal tyranny. Cardinal Cesare Baronius's twelve volumes of *Annales Ecclesiastici* (1588–1607) were intended as a comprehensive rebuttal of the Centuriators. Louis Sebastien le Nain de Tillemont published sixteen volumes of a *Memoire pour servir à l'histoire ecclesiastique des six premiers siecles* at Paris between 1693 and 1712 (it was for the best part of three centuries a major source for all patrologists).

23. On doctrinal radicalism in the period, see Maurice Wiles, *Archetypal Heresy. Arianism Through the Centuries,* Oxford, Clarendon Press, 1996, ch. 3; more generally, G. H. Williams, *The Radical Reformation,* 3rd edn, Kirksville, MO, 1992.

24. The best introduction to Petavius is still the article by P. Galtier in the *Dictionnaire de theologie catholique,* vol.xii/I, cols 1313–37.

25. On Bull, see L. W. Barnard, 'Bishop George Bull of St David's: Scholar and Defender of the Faith', *Journal of Welsh Ecclesiastical History* 9 (1992), pp. 37–51.

26. For further discussion of Johann Lorenz von Mosheim, see R. Williams,

'Newman's *Arians* and the Question of Method in Doctrinal History', in *Newman After a Hundred Years*, Ian Ker and Alan Hill (eds.), Oxford, Clarendon Press, 1990, pp. 263–285, especially 279–83.

27. A full study in E. P. Meijering, *Die Hellenisierung des Christentums im Urteil Adolf von Harnacks*, Amsterdam/Oxford/New York, North Holland Publishing Company, 1985. On Harnack more generally, W. Pauck, *Harnack and Troeltsch: Two Historical Theologians*, New York, Oxford University Press, 1968.

28. It is helpful to look at ch. 5 in vol. II of Bultmann's *Theology of the New Testament*, London, SCM Press, 1955, on this issue. Robert Morgan's article on 'Rudolf Bultmann' in *The Modern Theologians*, David Ford (ed.), Oxford, Blackwell, 1997, pp. 68–86, offers a good orientation on Bultmann himself and his influence on others (notably Ernst Käsemann, who more than shared Bultmann's critical attitude to 'early Catholicism'). See also Gareth Jones, *Bultmann. Towards a Critical Theology*, Oxford, Blackwell, 1991.

29. Elisabeth Schüssler Fiorenza, *In Memory of Her. A Feminist Theological Reconstruction of Christian Origins*, New York, Crossroad, 1983. This theme is brought out with great freshness and clarity by Roberta C. Bondi in her two books on the spiritual vision of the patristic era, *To Love as God Loves: Conversations with the Early Church*, Minneapolis, Augsburg/Fortress, 1987, and *To Pray and to Love: Conversations on Prayer with the Early Church*, Minneapolis, Augsburg/Fortress, 1991. I owe a special debt to these.

Chapter 2: RESIDENT ALIENS: THE IDENTITY OF THE EARLY CHURCH

1. For details of some local expressions of this, see S. R. F. Price, *Rituals and Power: The Roman Imperial Cult in Asia Minor*, Cambridge University Press, 1984. A more general study is Robin Lane Fox, *Pagans and Christians*, London, Viking, 1986, especially ch. 2.

2. Lane Fox, *op. cit.*, pp. 82–9, is of interest on this.

3. Related words appear in the New Testament at Eph. 2:19, and I Peter 1:17 and 2:11; c.f. Heb. 11:9. Compare the introduction to the account of Polycarp's martyrdom (a convenient translation in J. Stevenson (ed.), *A New Eusebius*, 2nd edn, London SPCK, 1960, no. 18) and the letter describing the martyrs of Lyons and Vienne (also in Stevenson, no. 21). On the 'resident alien' theme, see ch. 6 of Rowan A. Greer, *Broken Lights and Mended Lives. Theology and Common Life in the Early Church*, University Park and London, Pennsylvania State University Press, 1986.

4. Stevenson, *op. cit.*, no. 22.

5. For a recent discussion, see ch. 4 of Daniel Boyarin, *Dying for God. Martyrdom and the Making of Christianity and Judaism*, Stanford University Press, 1999.

6. Ignatius' Letter to the Romans, iv.

7. As above, n. 3.

8. Letter to Diognetus V; see Stevenson, *op. cit.*, no. 36.

9. The bishop in question was Callistus, his opponent Hippolytus; see

Hippolytus, *Refutation of All the Heresies*, IX.12. A recent study is A. Brent, *Hippolytus and the Roman Church in the Third Century*, Leiden, Brill, 1995.

10. The appeal to continence appears in Justin Martyr, *Apology*. xxix, Athenagoras, *Plea on Behalf of the Christians, xxxiii*. Eusebius refers to sexual continence as 'above nature' in his *Proof of the Gospel*, 1.8. On this subject in general, see Peter Brown, *The Body and Society. Men, Women and Sexual Renunciation in Early Christianity*, London, Faber, 1989, especially ch. 2 and ch. 3.

11. Stevenson, *op. cit.*, no. 200.

12. Peter Brown, *op. cit.*, ch. 7 and ch. 8; Boyarin, *op. cit.*, ch. 3, especially pp. 74–80, 86–92.

13. See ch. 1, n. 8.

14. Several examples in the Nag Hammadi texts: see *The Nag Hammadi Library*, James M. Robinson (trs.), Leiden, Brill, 1977, pp. 159, 213.

15. C.f. ch. 1, n. 7.

16. Amongst the vast literature on early Christian biblical interpretation, Frances Young, *The Art of Performance. Towards a Theology of Holy Scripture*, London, Darton, Longman and Todd, 1990, and *Biblical Exegesis and the Formation of Christian Culture*, Cambridge University Press, 1997, are particularly helpful.

17. See A. F. Segal, *Two Powers in Heaven. Early Rabbinic Reports about Christianity and Gnosticism*, Leiden, Brill, 1978, and William Horbury, *Jewish Messianism and the Cult of Christ*, London, SCM, 1998.

18. For a full survey, see R. P. C. Hanson, *The Search for the Christian Doctrine of God. The Arian Controversy 318–381*, Edinburgh, T. & T. Clark, 1988, especially ch. 1, ch. 3 and ch. 4, and R. Williams, *Arius: Heresy and Tradition*, 2nd edn, London, SCM, 2001.

19. Some of the key texts are to be found in Cyril of Alexandria's letters; see Cyril of Alexandria, *Select Letters*, Lionel R. Wickham (ed. and trs.), Oxford, Clarendon Press, 1983. pp. xxxi–xxxv of the introduction offer a good orientation on the issues.

20. This use of *theologia* to describe direct knowledge of God in adoration or contemplation goes back to Origen and is used by Eusebius, but is most clearly expressed by Evagrius of Pontus at the end of the fourth century. The famous saying in his treatise *On Prayer* ('If you are a theologian, you will pray truly. And if you pray truly, you are a theologian') is often quoted. See *The Philokalia*, vol. I, G. E. H. Palmer, Philip Sherrard and Kallistos Ware (ed. and trs.), London, Faber, 1979, p. 62, and c.f. the discussion by Diadochos of Photike, pp. 275 ff.

21. Philostorgius, who wrote in the early fifth century, is our major source from the non-Nicene side of the debate. There is a translation of Photius' summary of this document by E. Walford, London, Bohn, 1855.

22. Augustine's most important works against the Donatists are his treatise *On Baptism*, and Letter 185; the point about something more than complete external obedience and validity is touched on in Letter 93.

23. *On Baptism* III, xvi, on the importance of growth and advance, c.f. I.xv and VII.lii, and Letter 185.x.43 on the bonds of love and unity created by the Holy Spirit's continuing action.

24. Letter 185, ix.39 on the futility of using the Lord's Prayer if you believe that you are already pure and sinless.

25. The stress on love (the love brought to birth in us by the Holy Spirit) as the means of knowledge is echoed closely in, for example, *Confessions* VII.x.

26. See, for example, R. B. Eno, *The Rise of the Papacy*, Collegeville, Liturgical Press, 1990.

27. Hence his fierce disagreement from 255 to 257 with Stephen, Bishop of Rome. See Cyprian's Letters lxix, lxxi and lxxiv in particular, and for further discussion, Peter Hinchliff, *Cyprian of Carthage and the Unity of the Christian Church,* London, Chapman, 1974.

28. Eusebius, *Ecclesiastical History* VII. 2–9, especially 9 on Dionysius' recognition of someone who had apparently received baptism as a child outside the communion of the bishop in Alexandria.

29. A large part of Books VI and VII of Eusebius' history make up a kind of biography of Dionysius, utilising large numbers of his letters. VI.46 catalogues some of the more important items in the dossier not directly quoted.

30. Eusebius, *History* VII.11 for Dionysius, VIII.10 for Phileas.

31. For a first-class discussion of the themes of Barmen in their context and their significance in the work of Karl Barth, see Timothy Gorringe, *Karl Barth: Against Hegemony*, Oxford University Press, 1999, ch. 4, especially pp. 128–33.

32. On the continuities between Barmen and the Kairos declaration at Belhar in 1985, see Charles Villa-Vicencio (ed.), *On Reading Karl Barth in South Africa*, Grand Rapids, Eerdmans, 1988.

Chapter 3: GRACE ALONE: CONTINUITY AND NOVELTY IN THE REFORMATION ERA

1. There is a very nuanced discussion in Daniel Williams, 'Constantine, Nicaea and the "Fall" of the Church', Lewis Ayres and Gareth Jones (eds.), *Christian Origins. Theology, Rhetoric and Community*, London, Routledge, 1998, pp. 117–36, which refuses too easy a narrative of radical corruption as a result of Constantine's patronage.

2. It was used at the beginning of the synodical decree of the second Council of Nicaea in 787, for example, and caused great offence to the court theologians of Charlemagne in the West, who strongly criticised the formula in the *Libri Carolini*. For a very good account of these diverse views, see Judith Herrin, *The Formation of Christendom*, Oxford, Blackwell, 1987, pp. 417–24 and 434–9.

3. Thomas Gilby OP, *Principality and Polity. Aquinas an the Rise of State Theory in*

the West, London, Longmans, 1958, remains a sound guide to this aspect of St Thomas's thought; see especially ch.V.2 and ch.VI.4.

4. Debra Shuger, "'Societie Supernaturall": The Imagined Community of Hooker's *Lawes*' in A. S. McGrade (ed.), *Richard Hooker and the Construction of Christian Community*, Mediaeval and Renaissance Texts and Studies, Tempe, AZ, 1997, pp. 307–31, especially pp. 327–8.

5. The classic study remains J. Huizinga, *The Waning of the Middle Ages*, London, Pelican Books, 1955 (the first English edition was published in 1924), especially chs 12–14 and 17–18. Steven Ozment, *Protestantism. The Birth of a Revolution*, London, Fontana Press, 1993, pp. 33 ff. offers some caution about accepting Huizinga's version too uncritically, but allows the importance of his analysis of lay sentiments.

6. In 1513, Colet preached a Good Friday sermon attacking what we might now call pre-emptive military activity, and apparently questioning even 'just war'. Unfortunately, the King was at that moment preparing to invade France; Colet was persuaded personally by Henry to sanction the planned conflict (the story is told by Erasmus himself). See J. J. Scarisbrick, *Henry VIII*, London, Eyre and Spottiswoode, 1968, and Pelican Books, 1971, pp. 54–5.

7. One of the most significant texts is in the preface to the complete edition of Luther's Latin works, vol. 54 of the Weimar edition of Luther, pp. 185–6. The groundbreaking monograph by Gordon Rupp, *The Righteousness of God: Luther Studies*, London, Hodder and Stoughton, 1953, gives a comprehensive overview.

8. Hence Luther's insistence in the Heidelberg Disputation of 1518 on the centrality of encountering God in the cross – i.e. in the presence of the dereliction and suffering of God incarnate; and his association, in a letter of 1522, of the 'divine birth' in the soul with the experience of death and hell. See R. Williams, *The Wound of Knowledge. Christian Spirituality from the New Testament to St John of the Cross*, 2nd edn, London, Darton, Longman and Todd, 1990, ch. 7,and Alister McGrath, *Luther's Theology of the Cross*, Oxford, Blackwell, 1985. The Heidelberg Disputation can be found in vol. XVI of the Library of Christian Classics, *Luther: Early Theological Works*, James Atkinson (ed. and trs.), London, SCM Press, 1962.

9. See Daphne Hampson, *Christian Contradictions. The Structures of Lutheran and Catholic Thought*, Cambridge University Press, 2001, p. 57.

10. Hampson rightly notes (p. 14) that Luther can in one respect profess 'some kind of a "virtue ethics"', in that he sees the character of the person as determining the moral nature of an act; in this sense, theology determines ethics, not the other way around. But, granted the failure of most Catholic theologians to come to terms with Luther's uncompromisingly dialectical method, and granted the historically poor showing of Lutheran piety in generating a critical politics, it is still questionable whether we should conclude – as Hampson seems close to doing in her first chapter – that Lutheran theology is somehow inimical to any definition of virtue. Certainly it is

never a cause of justification; but it is not impossible to say how the action of Christ at work in the service of the justified person is to be identified.

11. For the English development, see Diarmaid MacCullough, *Tudor Church Militant. Edward VI and the Protestant Reformation*, London, Allen Lane, 1999, especially pp. 14–20. Ozment, *op. cit.*, ch. 6 on 'Luther's Political Legacy' is a useful guide.

12. Thomas Cartwright, the leading theologian of the Puritan party in the England of the 1570s and 1580s, argued this position in controversy with the future Archbishop Whitgift.

13. See John Bossy, *Christianity in the West 1400–1700*, Oxford University Press, 1985, pp. 153–61.

14. Pope John XXIII's encyclical *Pacem in Terris* (1963) and the Council's Pastoral Constitution *Gaudium et Spes* mark the transition to a new frame of reference.

15. Michel de Certeau, *The Mystic Fable. Volume One. The Sixteenth and Seventeenth Centuries*, University of Chicago Press, 1992, pp. 188–200, 292–9.

16. The contrast is between Andrewes' sermons on the anniversary of the Gunpowder Plot, in which he advocates extreme penalties against traitors, and, for example, his eloquent disavowal of violence by the Church in a Pentecost sermon of 1615 ('Sermon VIII of the Sending of the Holy Ghost', in Andrewes, *Ninety Six Sermons*, Oxford and London, James Parker, 1874, vol. III, pp. 245–64).

17. See R. Williams, 'Barth, War and the State', in Nigel Biggar (ed.), *Reckoning with Barth. Essays in Commemoration of the Centenary of Barth's Birth*, Oxford and London, Mowbray, 1988, pp. 170–90.

18. 'The Church of England has the satisfaction of knowing that it is training the generations on whom the future of the world depends' wrote Mandell Creighton in 1896 (Louise Creighton, *Life and Letters of Mandell Creighton*, vol. II, p. 175); c.f. ib. p. 395, 'I see no other home so well suited for a divine institution'. Examples could be multiplied. For the First World War, see Alan Wilkinson, *The Church of England and the First World War*, 2nd edn, 1996, London, SCM, especially p. 217 for Bishop Winnington Ingram's notorious sermon on the call 'to kill Germans … the good as well as the bad . . . lest the civilisation of the world should itself be killed.'

19. W. H. Auden, *Collected Poems*, London, Faber, 1976, p. 235.

20. Chs 7 to 9 of David Daniell, *William Tyndale. A Biography*, New Haven and London, Yale University Press, 1994, are of special interest. C.f. pp. xxv–xxix of Daniell's introduction to Tyndale's *The Obedience of a Christian Man*, London, Penguin, 2000.

21. This is not to say that Hooker is to be thought of strictly as a 'Reformed' theologian, as the detailed work of Nigel Voak (*Richard Hooker and Reformed Theology. A Study of Reason, Will, and Grace*, Oxford University Press, 2003) has shown. He is in many ways a very unorthodox Reformed thinker on the subject of grace; but in terms of his theology of the Church, he certainly seeks to sustain a mainstream Reformed position. See W. J. Torrance Kirby,

'Richard Hooker as an Apologist of the Magisterial Reformation in England' in A. S. McGrade (ed.), *Richard Hooker and the Construction of Christian Community,* Mediaeval and Renaissance Texts and Studies, Tempe Arizona, 1997, pp. 219–33, especially pp. 230–1.

22. Tyndale, *The Parable of the Wicked Mammon,* in the Parker Society edition of his works (Cambridge 1848), pp. 62–70, especially pp. 66–7 on duty to the poor, and pp. 93–9 on the unrestricted 'debt' owed to all in need, near or far.

23. See his sermon of 1586, 'A Learned Discourse of Justification, Works, and How the Foundation of Faith is Overthrown' (in John Keble's edition of Hooker's works, Oxford University Press, 1841, pp. 483–547), especially pp. 540–3.

24. ibid, pp. 518–24, 531ff.; c.f. the sermon 'Of the Certainty and Perpetuity of Faith in the Elect', ibid. pp. 469–81, especially pp. 470–5: if absolute subjective certainty about the things of God were available here below, would we not be saying that a person might be saved by the perfection of their knowledge (p. 471)? Our certainty is 'certainty of adherence' – that is, commitment to God as good (therefore desirable) not only as true.

25. See Kirby, n. 21 above.

26. For a good overview of these issues, see Patrick Collinson, 'Hooker and the Elizabethan Establishment', McGrade, *op. cit.,* pp. 149–81.

27. These included Hooker's own close associate, the Dutchman Hadrian Saravia, who fully accepted Episcopal *government* in the Church, but does not seem to have thought that this involved any necessity for Episcopal ordination.

28. See Dietrich Bonhoeffer, *The Way to Freedom. Letters, Lectures and Notes from the Collected Works,* London, Collins, 1966, pp. 75–96, especially pp. 80 (on the relation of baptism and being in communion), 93–4 (on separation from the Confessing Church as refusing salvation).

29. On theology and praise in general, see Daniel Hardy and David Ford, *Jubilate. Theology in Praise,* London, Darton, Longman and Todd, 1984. On hymns, see an outstandingly (if typically) arresting essay by David Martin, 'Music and Religion: Ambivalence Towards the Aesthetic', in his *Christian Language and its Mutations. Essays in Sociological Understanding,* London, Ashgate, 2002, pp. 47–67.

Chapter 4: HISTORY AND RENEWAL: THE RECORDS OF THE BODY OF CHRIST

1. London, SCM Press, 1993.

2. Ludwig Wittgenstein, *On Certainty,* Oxford, Blackwell, 1969. See also Stanley Cavell, *The Claim of Reason. Wittgenstein, Skepticism, Morality and Tragedy,* Oxford, Oxford University Press, 1979, Part 2.

3. Georges Florovsky, 'The Work of the Holy Spirit in Revelation', *The Christian East* 13, 1932, no. 2, pp. 49–64.

4. David Tracy, *The Analogical Imagination. Christian Theology and the Culture of*

Pluralism, London, SCM Press, 1981, ch. 3, has a helpful discussion of what a 'classic' is in this connection.

5. 'Someone said: "The dead writers are remote from us because we *know* so much more than they did." Precisely, and they are that which we know' (from the 1919 essay, 'Tradition and the Individual Talent', *Selected Prose of T. S. Eliot*, ed. Frank Kermode, London, Faber, 1975, pp. 37–44).

6. See, for example, Dimitris Kyrtatas, *The Social Structure of the Early Christian Communities*, London, Verso, 1987, esp. ch. 2.

7. For some cautions about concentrating only on what Christian language has in common with its milieu, see R. Williams, '"Is it the same God?" Reflections on Continuity and Identity in Religious Language', John H. Whittaker (ed.) *The Possibilities of Sense*, New York and Basingstoke, Palgrave, 2002, pp. 204–18, esp. 214–5.

8. A helpful, if slightly uncritical, recent introduction is Ralph McInerny, *The Very Rich Hours of Jacques Maritain: A Spiritual Life*, University of Notre Dame Press, 2003.

9. Henri de Lubac, *At the Service of the Church*, San Francisco, Ignatius Press, 1993, is a very personal account of this epoch by one of its greatest figures.

10. See R. Williams (ed.) *Sergeii Bulgakov: Towards a Russian Political Theology*, Edinburgh, T. & T. Clark, 1999, pp. 163–81, for some account of the intellectual quarrels in the Russian emigration over these matters.

11. This emerges clearly in McInerny, *op. cit.*, who observes how Maritain retained a significant degree of respect for Blondel and Bergson despite his intense arguments against them; to the degree that one can say that they helped substantially to form his own agenda.

12. His relatively brief but extremely influential work of 1944, translated into English in 1957 as *The Mystical Theology of the Eastern Church* (Cambridge, James Clarke), was an attempt at a synthesis of the main doctrinal themes of the Greek theologians of the fourth and fifth centuries. The themes were developed in a series of densely argued essays, published together posthumously and translated as *In the Image and Likeness of God*, Crestwood, St Vladimir's Seminary Press, 1974.

13. This paragraph summarises the arguments especially of chs 1, 5, 6 and 7 of *In the Image and Likeness of God*.

14. Etienne Gilson, whose influence on modern interpretations of Aquinas was probably even greater than that of Maritain (with whom he had important disagreements; McInerny, *op. cit.*, pp. 125–8), emphasised particularly this 'existentialist' element; see his magisterial work on *The Christian Philosophy of St Thomas Aquinas*, New York, Random House, 1956. The Anglican theologian Eric Mascall produced a very lucid development of this in books such as *Existence and Analogy*, London, Darton, Longman and Todd, 1966 (2nd edn).

15. See Fergus Kerr OP, 'French Theology: Yves Congar and Henri de Lubac' in David F. Ford (ed.) *The Modern Theologians: Introduction to Christian Theology in the Twentieth Century*, Oxford, Blackwell, 1997 (2nd edn), pp. 105–17.

16. *Paradoxes of Faith,* San Francisco, Ignatius Press, 1987, pp. 107–8.
17. There is a good balance of texts and a sensible introduction in *Celtic Spirituality*, translated and introduced by Oliver Davies with the collaboration of Thomas O'Loughlin, New York/Mahwah, Paulist Press (in the *Classics of Western Spirituality* series), 1999.
18. Chapter 29 of Peter Brown, *Augustine of Hippo: A Biography*, London, Faber, 1967, remains a fine summary; see also George Lawless, 'Augustine's Decentring of Asceticism' in Robert Dodaro and George Lawless (eds) *Augustine and His Critics,* London and New York, Routledge, 2000, pp. 142–63.
19. See John E. Booty, *John Jewel: An Apologist of the Church of England*, London, SPCK, 1963, p. 126 and ch. 6 *passim.*
20. Kierkegaard, *Philosophical Fragments/Johannes Climacus,* ed. and tr. Howard V. Hong and Edna H. Hong, Princeton University Press, 1985, pp. 66–71.
21. The issue has become a matter of some practical urgency in the Anglican Church of Australia, with pressure from the Diocese of Sydney to authorise lay presidency. Chs 5 and 6 of Peter Carnley, *Reflections in Glass,* New York and Sydney, HarperCollins, 2004, give some flavour of the debate. See also the report of the House of Bishops of the Church of England, *Eucharistic Presidency*, London, Church House Publications, 1997.
22. See the work of David Burrell in particular, most recently, *Faith and Freedom: An Interfaith Perspective,* Oxford, Blackwell, 2004; also *Catholics and Shi'a in Dialogue. Studies in Theology and Spirituality*, ed. Anthony O'Mahony, Wulstan Peterburs and Mohammed Ali Shomali, London, Melisende, 2004.
23. See, for example, Susan Walker (ed.) *Speaking of Silence. Christians and Buddhists on the Contemplative Way*, New York/Mahwah, Paulist Press, 1987.
24. Barbara Tuchmann, *A Distant Mirror: The Disastrous Fourteenth Century*, Harmondsworth, Penguin Books, 1979.
25. B. F. Westcott, *Lessons from Labour*, London, Macmillan, 1901, p. 148.
26. *Confessions* VII.10.
27. Ibid, p. xx.
28. The historian Jonathan Clark writes about the dangers of what he calls 'presentism', a dissolution of all historical perspective in the indifferent pluralism of postmodernity: 'By claiming to emancipate the present from the past, presentism promises to abolish the future also, for the future cannot look essentially different from that which we now have. The world ceases to be a narrative of suffering and achievement, and becomes a timeless shopping mall . . . Past generations cease to relate to future generations, since past generations did not shop in the same mall. Future generations will raise no problems of difference or continuity, since, it is presumed, they will continue to shop there.' (J. C. D. Clark, *Our Shadowed Present: Modernism, Postmodernism and History*, London, Atlantic Books, 2003, p. 28.)

INDEX

Abraham 8, 29
Acton, Lord 11, 24
Africa 34–5, 49, 51
analogy 102–3
Andrewes, Lancelot 73
Anglican Communion 56, 85
Anglicanism 11, 21–2, 50, 73, 79, 82, 102, 106
Anglo-Saxons 17
Anselm, St 98
anti-Semitism 54
Antichrist 19
apartheid 54–5, 85
apostles 8–9, 11
Arian Controversy 15
Arius 14–15, 43–4
Asia Minor 13
Auden, W. H. 74
Augustine of Hippo 15–16, 20, 49–50, 53, 72, 87, 102, 112
authority 104–5, 109, 111

Babylon 6
Barmen Declaration 54–6
Baronius, Cardinal 20
Barth, Karl 73, 98
Becket, St Thomas 61
Bede 16–19, 23
Bergson, Henri 98
Bible 6, 11, 13, 26, 28–9
  in early Church 42

  in Reformation 63, 65–6, 69, 78, 80, 84, 86–7
bishops 14, 39, 49, 51–2, 81, 93
Bishops of Rome see Popes
Blondel, Maurice 98
Bonhoeffer, Dietrich 84–6
Britain 17, 73, 88
British Empire 73
Buddhist tradition 109
Bull, Bishop George 22
Bultmann, Rudolf 23, 26
Byzantium 18, 60, 102

Cain 9
Cajetan, Cardinal 66
Calvinism 21, 68–9, 77, 81, 98
Canterbury Cathedral 55
Carmelite tradition 71–2
Catholic tradition 4, 11, 17, 18, 20–3, 25, 55, 63, 66–7, 69–71, 73–4, 77, 80, 82, 84, 97–8, 100–1, 106
Celtic Christianity 102–3
Certeau, Michel de 71
Chalcedon, Council of 45, 56
Christology 57
Civil War, English 81, 102
cold war 73
Colet, Dean 63
Confessing Church 54, 57–8, 84–5
Constantine, Emperor 14, 60

Counter-Reformation 69, 71
Creighton, Mandell 11
culture wars 56, 111–12
Cybele 33
Cyprian, St 51

Davies, Norman 5
Decius, Emperor 38
Descartes, René 72
Diocletian, Emperor 13–14
Dionysius of Alexandria 51–2
Donatism 48, 50
Dutch Reformed Church of
   South Africa 85

ekklesia 34, 37, 46, 48, 56
Eliot, T. S. 94
Elizabeth I, Queen 69, 79, 104
England 5, 68, 73, 75, 78, 81–2
English tradition 17–18
Enlightenment 72, 87
Erasmus, Desiderius 63
Eusebius of Caesarea 12–15,
   17–19, 23, 25–6, 28, 44, 47, 52,
   104
existentialism 98

feminism 25–6, 28
First World War 73, 98
Florovsky, Georges 98
Foxe, John 19, 26
France 21
Francis of Assisi 18

Gaul 93
Germany 22–3, 54, 57–8, 73,
   84–5, 98
Gildas 17
gnostic traditions 19, 40–1, 44,
   103
Greek Fathers 43, 98–101

Hastings, Battle of 4–5
Hebrew Scripture 6–7, 9, 40, 43,
   51
Hegel, G. W. F. 98
Henry II, King 61
Henry VIII, King 63
Holy Roman Empire 62
Holy Spirit 29, 49, 84
Hooker, Richard 75, 77–9
hymnody 86, 92

idolatry 7, 58, 68, 88
Ignatius of Antioch, St 36, 52
Incarnation 21
Indonesia 5
Islam 109, 113
Israel 51, 68
Italy 21, 62, 93

Jerusalem 7–8
Jesuits 21
Jesus 7–8, 12, 29, 35, 40–5
Jewel, John 104
John of the Cross, St 71
Judaism 6–7, 9, 12–13, 33, 43–4,
   51, 109
Judea 6
Julian, Emperor 15

Kairos Document 54
Kant, Immanuel 72
Kierkegaard, S. 98, 105
Knox, Ronald 4

Letter to Diognetus 37
Lossky, Vladimir 98–100
Lubac, Henri de 101
Luther and Lutheranism 9, 57,
   63, 65–8, 71–8, 80–2, 84, 86–7,
   93

MacIntyre, Alasdair 47
Magdeburg, Centuries of 20
Maritain, Jacques 98
Markus, Robert 15
martyrdom 11, 14, 19, 34–7,
  39–40, 44, 53, 55–7, 59–60, 92,
  111
Marxism 113
misogyny 97
Mithras 33
Moses 8
Mosheim, J. L. von 22

New Testament 6–8, 23, 34, 43,
  87
Nicene Creed 21–2, 45, 47, 50,
  56, 104
Nineham, Dennis 89
Numidia 34

Old Testament 6–9, 12, 17, 19, 68
Origen 13–14
Orthodoxy, Eastern 55, 92, 97–8

paganism 15, 19, 55, 102
Palestine 5
Pelagius 50, 102–3
Paul 27, 98
persecution 13–14, 19, 38–9, 47
Petau, Denis (Petavius) 21–2
Pharisaism 38
Phileas of Thmuis 53
Pietism 23
Pius V, Pope 69
Plantagenets 5
Plato 22
Poland 21
Polycarp, St 35–6, 38, 42, 44,
  46–7, 52, 55
Popes 11, 21, 37, 62–3, 65, 68–9,
  80

Protestantism 19–22, 37, 63, 66,
  70, 73, 76, 78–81
Puritanism 78–9

Rabbinic tradition 43
Reformation 18–20, 22–3, 25,
  30, 50, 59–88, 90, 93, 97, 111
Reformed Churches 57, 68, 71,
  73–8, 80–2, 84–5, 104
Renaissance 11, 62
Roman Empire 11–12, 15, 17,
  32–8, 44, 53–4, 60
Rome 8, 17, 19, 37, 51, 61, 92,
  102
Rome, Bishop of see Popes
Russia 98–9

Schüssler Fiorenza, Elisabeth 23,
  26
Scilli, martyrs of 34–5
second power 43
Second Vatican Council 70
secularisation 62
serpent 9
Shuger, Debra 62
Silver Age 98
slavery 97
South Africa 54–5, 85
Syrian tradition 102

Teresa of Avila 71
Third Reich 54–5, 57
Thomas Aquinas 61, 98, 100–1
Tillemont, L. A. Le Nain de 20
transparency 107–9
Trent, Council of 69, 71, 81,
  84–5
Trinity 21, 45, 83, 96, 99–100
Tyndale, William 75–9, 86

Unitarianism 22–3

virginity 39–40, 44
Von Harnack, Adolf 22

Westcott, Bishop 112
Westminster Abbey 55

Whigs 61
Wittgenstein, Ludwig 90
World Alliance of Reformed
    Churches 85